YELLOW
SILK

yellow

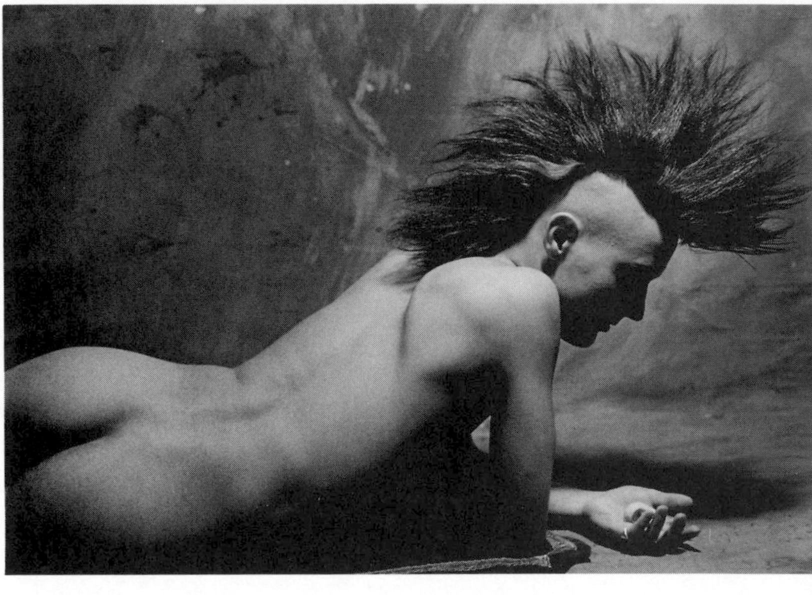

SILK

EROTIC

ARTS

AND

LETTERS

Edited by

LILY POND AND RICHARD RUSSO

Harmony Books ☿ New York

Book design by Nancy Kenmore

Published by Harmony Books, a division of Crown Publishers, Inc., 201 East 50th Street, New York, New York 10022. Member of the Crown Publishing Group. For more information on *Yellow Silk: Journal of the Erotic Arts*, please contact Yellow Silk, P.O. Box 6374, Albany, California 94706.

HARMONY and colophon are trademarks of Crown Publishers, Inc.

Manufactured in the United States of America

Library of Congress Cataloging-in-Publication Data

Yellow silk : erotic arts and letters / edited by Lily Pond and
    Richard A. Russo. — 1st ed.
        p.   cm.
    1. Erotic literature.   I. Pond, Lily.   II. Russo, Richard A.
    (Richard Anthony), 1946–
PN6071.E7Y45   1990
810.8'03538—dc20   90-4548
                                                                        CIP

ISBN 0-517-57752-6

10 9 8 7 6 5 4 3 2 1

First Edition

CONTENTS

LIST OF ILLUSTRATIONS

P R E F A C E ▪ *The Magazine*

hen I began *Yellow Silk* nine years ago, it never occurred to me that nearly everyone would ask, "What's the difference between erotic and pornographic?" But since everyone has, I'll assume you're wondering too and will answer you up front.

Pornography, that by which American society is purportedly so frightened, is really a very shallow thing. It is predictable, unchallenging, and utilitarian; its clear results are profit (for the producer) and arousal (for the consumer). Its very predictability makes it controllable and therefore not really very frightening.

It is the erotic that is most genuinely terrifying. Though it is often incomprehensible, it is the basic binding force of the universe. It is powerful, attractive, and wondrous—and embodies all that empowers our beings with emotion and passion, all that spills over the boundaries and infuses us with life.

Ironically, it is Eros that is also often the most subtle. It is the thought before the idea, the shadow behind the screen. While it may be the cackling in the wee hours of the morning, and the dancing before the moon, it is also the glance in the sunlight, the red hair across an arm: It *makes* you stop and feel; it works its way gradually; it allows no defenses; it is irresistible.

Yes, we are seeing the erotic when we see people making love, but we are also seeing it in the birth moment of a child, the tense pressured budding of a tree, the creation of a brilliant painting, in the genesis of all poetry, in the mystic vision of the mad priest (or the sane one). It is in everything that releases us from the restraints of everyday civilization and makes us free.

But, frankly, I've also always thought that the question was inappropriate. What I publish in *Yellow Silk* is literature and art; this isn't work created *to be erotic*, this is work—fiction, poetry, paintings, photographs—created as all art is created, through that mysterious process, one might even call it an erotic process, based on *need* on the part of the creator. Like the root that breaks the walk—there is no holding it back. The relevant question here is not whether or not it "turns you on," and if so, does it do it in some tasteful and politically correct manner. No, the question is, does it make your heart beat or your ears ring? Does it blow off the top of your head? Whatever the criteria you bring to art, do you bring it to this? Does it satisfy?

When I started this magazine, I never dreamed that this would be confusing to people. Although contemporary American culture seemed to assume that Eros has no legitimate place in literature or the fine arts, I was convinced this simply wasn't true. Many other past and present cultures—Japan, France, and India among them—have integrated the erotic into their arts. Why should even the idea be so nearly inconceivable here?

When I sought out small-press and literary magazines available in this country, I found work far more somber, more drawn from the intellect than the paintings, poems, and stories I'd always most loved: Chagall, Gauguin, Utamaro, and all of the Art Nouveau designers; Rimbaud, Nabokov, Shange, Ihara, and Kotzwinkle—all of these magicians brought music, color, passion and, frequently, sexuality to their work. What I found published there often had, and I mean this *literally*, death in the first paragraph. Well, as Mary Mackey asks elsewhere in this book, if death were legitimate, why then not life?

Yet years later, here I am. Maybe I was right after all. Perhaps it is possible for a public to accept that sexual writing can be literature, if it is brilliantly written. Perhaps it is possible for people to see that Eros manifests itself identically in all loving relations, whatever the gender or sexual persuasion may be; perhaps there are still many people who find the dragon-hip leather and studs of current fashion to have nothing whatever to do with the genuine nature of Eros. I never dreamed an anthology in your hands, either.

yellow

Though I sometimes have to drag myself to the work-table, once there, I'm so often rewarded; imagine finding an exquisite, perfect poem, or a story that is so gorgeously written you have to call up the author immediately and thank him or her for sending it to you. Imagine seeing a painter's work that is exactly what you've been looking for, and not only do you have an artist for your next issue, but you also have a new friend. Imagine a vehicle through which to show your favorite story to fifteen thousand or so people. Imagine a vehicle that brings new favorites in the mail. (Imagine also *picking* from all those favorites for this book; thanks enormously to Richard Russo for accepting the jealous task I never could perform.)

So, this is *Yellow Silk*. It's a group of ideas, feelings, images gathered together in particular ways four times a year to make issues called, for example, "The Music of Eros," "Japonisme," or "Domesticity." These stories, poems, and artworks are woven into a whole that is, in and of itself, something that stands alone. Perhaps it is even silken.

Consider yourself introduced. This is the four children I've had yearly for nearly a decade. This is the pigeon flock I've fed on the roof in all weathers. This is the daughter I drove to ballet recital and the son I picked up from little league—and vice versa. This is the lover for whom I went out on the rainy night for hot Chinese food; this is the lover who warmed me with stories when I was ill and couldn't sleep. In short, the magazine's my life, but we bring each other our best and our all.

Bring the best of yourself, too. At least as well as you can. I know she won't disappoint. For this is also the lover who knows all your best places, and knows how you most like them treated.

This book is dedicated to the peoples around the world who at this writing are also finding their dreams come most unexpectedly true; and to Wu and the Pooh, without whom this book would not have happened. Further thanks to Bruce Harris and Kathy Belden at Crown Publishers, without whose persistence, patience, and foresight we'd probably still be peddling orange juice out on the corner. Lastly, thanks to *all* of the writers and artists who've been in *Yellow Silk* over the years, and to everyone who's worked on the magazine in that time. Without them we simply would not have flown.

LILY POND

yellow

INTRODUCTION

*S*ince 1981, *Yellow Silk: Journal of Erotic Arts* has been seeking out and publishing work that recognizes, honors, and
explores an aspect of life that has been distorted and di-
minished in our culture, an aspect represented in Western
mythology by Eros, the God of Love. More than just sexual
energy, Eros is the Life Force itself: the joyous, exuberant, ex-
pansive energy that flows through all things and includes
sexuality as one of its aspects.

In this anthology you will find many pieces that can be
considered "erotic" in the narrow sense of the word—stories like
Decarnin's "The Dozen Kisses" or Underwood's "Zulu Warrior," poems like Hacker's *Then* or Weitzman's *after reading John
Updike's poem entitled 'Cunts.'* But you will also find work that
challenges and expands conventional notions of the erotic. In
Olsen's story, "Augustine's Last Days," Eros flourishes amidst
the world's worst horrors; in Roggenbuck's "Estelle's Death"
and St. Aubin's "Cynthia," it triumphs over death. Stories like
Covina's "There Are Flowers for Everyone in These Hills" or
Wood's "Organic Gardening" exuberantly affirm the body's connection to the earth, while Hirshfield's poem, *Percolation*, takes
us even further, showing how Eros flows through and connects
all things and concluding that "surely all Being at bottom is
happy."

Clearly, we are not talking about what is commonly
called "erotica." Erotica is writing and art that is only about
sex; its aim is to arouse. In contrast, the typical *Yellow Silk*
piece touches the heart and the mind as well as the genitals; it
may concern sex, but it is ultimately about life, and the power
within us that gives forth all hope and passion and connection
and joy.

In *Pornography and Silence*, Susan Griffin, discussing the
"knowledge of the body" that has been denied by culture but

can be rediscovered through erotic feeling, describes it this way: ". . . to touch another is to express love; there is no idea apart from feeling, and no feeling which does not ring through our bodies and our souls at once. This is Eros. Our own wholeness. Not the sensation of pleasure alone, nor the idea of love alone, but the whole experience of human love. The whole range of human capacity exists in this love."

Or, as Rollo May put it in *Love and Will*, "We are in Eros not only when we experience our biological, lustful energies, but also when we are able to open ourselves and participate, via imagination and emotional and spiritual sensitivity . . . in the interpersonal world and the world of nature."

This anthology gathers together my choices from the first eight years of *Yellow Silk:* fiction, poetry, and art that opens the heart and turns on the mind as well as the body. I've taken care to include the authors and artists who have been most closely associated with the magazine, and also to present a variety of forms and voices that is representative of the range of work that has appeared in *Yellow Silk*.

The book is divided into sections, but not in any obvious way. Instead of grouping pieces together that have similar subject matter, we've combined work of different but complementary tones, voices, and themes. A quote chosen from one of the pieces, together with a piece of art that has appeared in the magazine, sounds an opening note for each sequence. In this way, each section is like a typical issue of the magazine in miniature. In addition, the sections vary in length and tone, so that the book as a whole has a musical rhythm when read straight through: a hymn in celebration of Eros.

RICHARD A. RUSSO

"There Are Flowers

For everyone in
These HILLS"

HOW IT FEELS #11

■

Roberta Werdinger

This time, holding the vulva open hard with my hand and feeling wild deer bound out of it.

YOUR CROTCH IN THE MORNING AFTER MAKING LOVE ALL NIGHT AFTER NOT SEEING YOU FOR ALL SUMMER HAIKU

■

Jeffrey Wilson

The yellow autumn
meadow damp from September's
three o'clock cloud burst.

yellow

THERE ARE FLOWERS FOR EVERYONE IN THESE HILLS

∎

Gina Covina

There are flowers for everyone in these hills. There are flowers, in May, to suit every fancy. There are monkey flowers, and butter and eggs; Chinese houses and purple nightshade; redwood sorrel and colt's foot and mule's ear and goat's beard. There are twenty-five different clovers in residence in Sonoma County, though they may not all be in flower today. There are milk maids and sugar scoops and sun cups and angelica. There are Solomon's seals both slim and fat, and false Solomon's seal as well. There are rare flowers: the redwood lily, the lady's slipper, the stream orchis, the ghost-white phantom orchid. For the moon and the moody there are baneberry, witches' teeth, skullcap. There is death camas looking like the edible wild onion. There is Ithuriel's spear. There is Diogenes' lantern.

In the hills the fairies are at their most active, dancing in the flowers night and day, ensouling each bloom as it moves from bud to bee-food. Zorra Beth wanders the deer trails in sunlight, picking bouquets for the table, for the outhouse, for her mother's beauty salon. She wears white, these days, and walks barefoot. Fern fronds and meadow foam make a crown in her hair. Frank O'Flanrahan sees her as he comes into the hills with a big basket to pick wild greens for the dinner salad. They wind their ways across the hillside slowly, like forager bees making as many stops as there are flowers. They pass each other twice, three times, gathering.

Buttercup, brodiaea, blue-eyed Mary. Shepherd's purse, plantain, chickweed, dock. Zorra Beth walks softly; she sniffs a dozen flowers for every one she touches; she touches many before picking one. Frank holds a sharp knife, and the basket on his arm. He crouches and cuts, walks and crouches, cuts and gazes—at the bright sky, at the new green, at the floating cloud hem of Zorra Beth's dress, passing.

■

Bees are working the flowers. Honeybees and bumblebees and sugar bees and little flies. The bees' honey stomachs are full; the back legs of the pollen gatherers hang down heavy-weighted. Zorra Beth's heart floods the hillside with her particular yellow-white joy. Frank feels it, watching her; his own blue-white light spreads through Zorra Beth's yellow, making a green-white that could easily be mistaken for the souls of the springtime plants, rising. Frank catches Zorra Beth's eye, and they pause a moment to look into each other. Neither one holds anything back; neither one smiles.

California poppy provides the thick scattered orange, and the texture of silk. Bush monkey flower brings in yellow, and velveteen. Vetch and lupine color the hillside in violets that slide from pale pink to deep purple. Blue-eyed grass reflects the sky; yarrow holds up stalks of white; buttercups mirror the sun, and Indian paintbrush flings bright red across the meadow—all of this shimmering on the deep green of May, all of it alive with bees and butterflies, all shimmering, all alive. Frank stashes his knife and basket of greens in the shade of a bush lupine, and spreads himself into a dish of the meadow, arms out wide and face to the blue. He doesn't see Zorra Beth set her flowers down beside his basket; he doesn't hear her bare feet moving through the green. He doesn't see her reach down to catch the hem of her dress in her hands; doesn't see her stretch her arms over her head and remove the dress in one smooth gesture; doesn't hear the white cotton drop to the ground. Frank doesn't know she is there until she is stretched out along his length, suddenly, all her warm weight pressing into him, her skin dazzling white in the sunlight, her breath on his chin, her bright small eyes on his.

"Zorra Beth." It is all he can say, and softly, as his hands slowly move along the curving warmth of her skin.

yellow

Zorra Beth doesn't say anything. Not one small joke, not one witty sentence, not even a murmured sentimental endearment or a giggle at the surprise in Frank's eyes. She doesn't even smile. She sits up, straddling him, and begins to unbutton his shirt. Slowly, all of it slowly, with the May sun warm across her back and framing her face in gold as the light catches in her hair.

A bee works in the clover an inch from Frank's left ear. A small black ant crosses Zorra Beth's foot. Frank watches a translucent pale spider pause at Zorra Beth's shoulder, as she reaches to pull off his shoes; as she turns back, to unzip his pants, the spider slants off into the meadow sun, following some invisible thin thread of its own making. Frank lifts his hips so Zorra Beth can pull off his trousers. There are flowers for everyone in these hills.

POEM

■

Roberta
Werdinger

Give me your blood your bone
your sockets your breath
Give me the precise surge of your capillaries
your hands which are pretending to be fish
Give me your gaze which sweetens rainwater
Give me the wind that blows down your thighbone
Let me drink the fluid that cushions your brain
Show me the light which streams from your fingernails
Give me the snow that collects beneath your cheekbone
the animals behind your teeth,
waiting
Give me the impulses wired in your hair
your arms which are antennae
Give me the starlings that crouch in your shoulders
and the swallows that sleep in your feet
Give me the grasses in your eyebrows
Show me the tunnel your eyes are made of

Come hover on my brain as a bee to a flower
Run your finger down the blackness behind my ribcage
Make a puzzle of my womb
an alphabet of my fingers
Paste me to the ceiling of the underworld
Show me the solemn procession of the intestines
Lead me into the creek of my blood cells
Open my body leave in a mark
Open me river me do what you will.

"I WANT YOU

WITH THREE
MOUTHS"

AFTER READING JOHN UPDIKE'S POEM ENTITLED "CUNTS"

■

*Sarah Brown
Weitzman*

spreading wider
his concept of beauty
to include that part of women
not considered beautiful before
he fingers that
idea and comes in
and out of irony
still he tells
of a beauty
of this second mouth
much as I would say
of my man's member
first like a fig
wrinkled and ringed
cushioned in repose
on uneven corrugated sacks
that soon will swing and bang
against that part of me
even D. H. Lawrence skipped
describing where his love is laid
and where that lady shits

this limp part
of love
which flutters like a live bird
in my hand
before it is locked
in the damp cage
of myself
draws hard
from me
my tensions
and seeks my secret
fantasies
and gets them

yellow

that part of men
little mentioned
in women's poetry before this age
rises like an idea in me
giving as much as taking
leading me on
to more than one discovery
so that always each time now
whenever I see you
like a muse
nude and renewing
I want you
with three mouths

THE DOZEN KISSES

■

C. M. Decarnin

She passes him where he's leaning against a wall on Polk Street with three other boys. Pretty soon she walks back and leans against the wall next to him.

—Hi.

He nods. He looks into her eyes very steadily.

—Nice day, she adds.

—Yeah.

—What's your name?

—Ken.

—How old are you?

—Sixteen.

—Sure.

He shrugs.

—You want to go for a walk?

—Where?

—I thought you might know a good place.

He looks a little uncertain.

—It depends . . .

—How much to go indoors somewhere?

—Well, forty dollars plus—you mean like a room?—plus the room then.

She takes money out of her jeans.

—Hm. Haven't got it.

She smiles.

—How much for a kiss?

She notices him glancing up and down the street quickly.

—Can they bust you for a kiss? Jesus. Well, live dangerously.

They are both aware of the other three boys, who are watching the passers-by relentlessly.

yellow

—So how much for a kiss?

He grins a little and cocks his head back.

—First one's free.

She laughs. She leans toward him and he backs off, then stops.
She kisses his lips very gently.

—And the second?

—Oh now that'll cost you.

—Yes?

She sees a flicker of embarrassment in his eyes.

—How about a dollar? That's probably standard church bazaar
price. She peels one off the stack and gives it to him. He puts
it in his front jeans pocket.

She kisses him again, more lingeringly.

She gives him another dollar and this time puts her hand on his
shoulder while she kisses him, and just touches the lowest curls
of his hair against his neck. He looks again up and down the
street. Two men passing look away. She checks out the street
too. Then she steps out to face him, plants a boot on each side
of his sneakers, and slowly pulls another dollar loose. She folds
it, and tucks it with two fingers deep into his jeans pocket.
Leaning in, she finds his mouth again. Her tongue rolls slowly
over his lips. The tip flutters between and he opens to her. She
pulls back slowly.

—God damn, she says softly.

She puts another bill in his pocket.

One hand on the wall at either side of him, she lets her thighs
touch his, her pelvis press what's in his jeans, her belly lean in
against him while she kisses with her tongue slowly thrusting
deep in and out of his warm, wet mouth.

—Hey, he says.

—I didn't do anything but kiss you.

—The hell you didn't.

But he keeps his half-closed eyes on hers. She takes the five
from her dwindling stack.

SILK

—I won't lay a hand on you.

With a steady smile she puts the end of the rolled bill under the edge of his pocket and delicately taps it down in with the end of one finger. His shoulders are against the wall, his curly hair spread on the brick. This time when her mound nudges his crotch, there's more there. She pulls back slightly and with a soft intake of breath he pushes close against her. Her return weight moves his buttocks back onto the wall, but then she removes herself subtly from the proper contact—he finds it again, and rubs. This kiss falls on his neck near the shoulder. It strays by millimeters till he sinks down slightly along the wall, pressing out harder at the hips. Then it takes on an edge of teeth. His breath comes out in pieces.

She pushes the delicious numbness in her crotch up against his ridge a moment—then breaks away. He opens his eyes. She looks into them, breathing raggedly.

—How many is that?

—How many what?

She smiles delightedly.

—One, she tells him.

—One, he repeats.

She kisses his panting mouth and he struggles for breath around her tongue. She shoves up and down on his bulge, keeping her mouth open and breathing through it, but with her tongue lying on his. The rhythm of their breaths in each other's mouths heats her. Then she feels his tongue move—around, up over hers, into her mouth. It's very soft. She closes her lips gently as she lets her breasts touch the buttons of his shirt pockets. She feels she is surrounding his whole body, small and strong and pushing against the trap her thighs and arms make, without wanting to get free, but only be more securely prisoned. Wet runs out of her. When she notices that the three boys have moved between them and the sidewalk she pumps harder at him. Her legs are spread too far, around his, she realizes. Just

yellow

then she feels his hand working between them. She shrinks
back to let it pass, clamps it tight, gives way again. Finally she
feels small fingers paddling in her crotch. They don't hit critical
spots but the fact that they are there makes her hump harder.
His hand twists, and cups his own genitals, perhaps pro-
tectively. The added bulk between them gives her the ex-
crescence she needs. She feels the change in her cunt that is
like the difference between warm sun and heat lightning. She
abandons his mouth, gasps air, and wriggles herself urgently on
the hard bumps of his knuckles. She builds quickly—she comes:
globular lightning in her groin implodes; rebounds, sheets out
over her whole body and jerks it like a puppet. She presses
home and milks long surges of pleasure from her cunt. Finally
she makes herself lean back. She laughs. The whole episode has
been carried off silently, without much obvious movement, the
way she learned to do it in the dorm. Often men—and
women—don't even know when she's come. But the boy is
looking at her: he knows.
—Now how many?
—Two? he mumbles incredulously.
She pushes herself against his hand again.
—No, don't move, she says. It's good that way.
He moves his fingertips under his balls, and pushes out against
her. Her mouth drops onto his collarbone while she applies herself again to his fist. She lets her tonguetip slide slowly down
toward his tit, and he arches a little sideways, giving the lightest moan. At that, all her hip muscles tighten. She prods at
him rapidly and in fifteen seconds the heat of her cunt coalesces
again, makes her stop her breath and squeeze onto him, orgasm
bringing a ferocious tenderness; she wants to run hands hard
down his back, capture his ass and hug him into her, clasp
him, carry him to the ground— She staggers a step back and,
—Three, he says, reaching for her, with a hand that turns
timid at the touch of her flannel shirt. But she can feel the light

pressure on her flank and leans again upon him. She buries her
lips in his curls, licks into the roots of his hair as she rubs off.
There is a faint smoky smell to his hair; she wonders where he
spent the night, and at the quick images comes. She wonders if
men fuck into him, and if he comes then, or not. She presses
him hard into the brick. She is breathing heavily when she
throws her head back.

—Four, he gasps, and his hand drops to her ass and presses her
still in. She continues rubbing, and feels his other hand under
her, faster. The alien rhythm excites her, she sets up a sideways counterpoint. With a faint cry covered by the traffic
noise, he arches hard between her thighs, again and again, and
she closes her teeth on his lower lip. Another cry lifts her to
the finality of his intervals. All her muscles stiffen, she tremors,
and as he comes, breath cracking in his throat, she feels herself
against a field of stars, of sparklers, of firework fountains. She
grinds her teeth back and forth on his lip and he spasms help-
lessly; she lets his mouth go, fucks on him while he rises to
her. He gasps shallowly, with closed eyes.

—Yes! she hisses. Yes—

And comes. He sags and she catches him to her a moment, scrap-
ing a knuckle on the wall, still pulsing. There is a smell of come
between them. As he gets his feet again she divides her last two
dollars, putting one in her own pocket and holding one to him.

—How about special rates for a steady customer. Two for the
price of one?

He gives a breathy laugh, part disbelief, and takes the green
paper.

A small patch on his jeans, surprisingly off to one side, shows
wet.

They both look carefully up and down the street. But something of their own private universe still clings, behind the
screen of the other three hustlers. She feels the spot on the wall
warm from his body. One arm around him, she leans there,
and kisses his cheek.

yellow

—How old are you really?

—Fourteen. She gazes at him. —Practically.

She sighs.

—*Certified* jailbait.

—They wouldn't do anything to a woman.

He is still panting a little.

—Like hell they wouldn't.

—Serve you right for ripping off an innocent little kid.

—"Ripping off"? You were paid handsomely for those kisses.

—"Kisses."

—I've still got one more coming.

The three other boys suddenly drift apart and walk toward the ice cream parlor two doors up. He pulls away from her and starts walking. She walks beside him, hoping that to the two cops across and down the street she will look like a mother or maiden aunt, girlfriend.

—So I'll take a rain check.

Looking over, she memorizes his eyes, of the lightest green, and the wildly curly hair that is a dark powdery spade-blond, his complexion almost the same shade.

The two cops walk by.

—This must be a scary way to live.

—*Sometimes*, he says pointedly, —more than others.

—Next time I'll bring enough for a room. Are you here a lot?

—Only when I need money.

Irony.

She steers him around the corner onto Sutter, looks both ways, and puts her arms around him.

—The hell with rain checks. They hug gently and it is he who turns his mouths to hers.

—You're terrific, she murmurs. —Don't let anybody tell you different.

She walks away, looking back once and waving.

SILK

SPEAK OF IT

■

*Jane
Underwood*

opened

the cheeks, the chin, the nose
after a moment
shifted to one side
biting her ears

she laughed, nervous
her shoulders, her breasts
in the past

he leaned over
looking at her

then opened her

boundaries

part of her thighs

the steps
of a house

all
speak of it

the clitoris

the skin
between pubis and ass

a low
nearly palpable tone

forming the syllables
little girl

the gate

house

the house speaks
under the undercurve

yellow

slow
revolvings

rich odor
of the shadowy

sun-warmed
black curls
lying flat

silence

moving past them
the heated, active
silence

upon which
each imprinted
the insistent flame

to find
that singular
impersonal
salt

entrance

and in one instant
the mountains
opening in her chest

a wind
a blaze of white
circling the bedpost

all the wings
in her startled bones
waking and talking
the whole night

SILK

voice

undid
hips

pulled
the string

began
to rise

a voice
and the voice breaking
from its dark basket

consecrated

he was
darkly
bending her
to the ground

cold bits of cheese
and moon

the timbre of it
entering

into her narrow
whirl and grunt

"THe one WITH

miLKY THIGHS..."

FIONA MCNAIR

■

*Cerridwen
Fallingstar*

Like every loss of innocence, it started innocently enough. We were twelve, brash hooligans wild as lynx or lark or the unpredictable spring storms. We were still not above stealing the horse-shoes over someone's barn or tying elf-locks in their horses' manes and tails. We could be thoughtful, leaving bunches of flowers on people's doorsteps. On the other hand, we were just as likely to leave a basket of snails. Early April, the ground already thawing. Annie's cat had just had kittens.

Up in the loft, tickling each other into hysteria rolling off the blanket into the hay, yellow prickles in our hair, "Ow! Stop yer silliness!" giggles snickers snorts horsey smells in our noses. "You be the kitten an' I'll be Tawny," you say. "If yer the mumcat where are yer teats?" Russet kitten I become, pawing through your clothes in search of milk. I find your slight breast and latch on. Your turn to cry out and cuff me. "Ow, damn kitten, I think yer father was a robber lynx! Coory doon bairn 'tis time fer yer bath." I make no protest as she undresses me. We've slept and played naked together often, to both our mothers' distress. "Gypsy brat!" her mother would screech at her when Annie palmed the bannocks or rifled her purse, or cut up her clothes into costumes no decent person would wear. Everyone expected Annie to be bad since her father was a wicked thieving gypsy. Bad she was.

But what a sweet tongue she had. Not rough like Tawny's, so smooth and warm. My skin rumpled into goose-prickles along the paths her tongue left wet to the air. But who would complain? This shivering was different from any I'd ever known, quivering in such a strange way that even as my skin prickled I got warmer and warmer. The between-my-legs part felt the most shivery of all. As she moved from my breast to my ribs across my belly I knew that I wanted her to put her mouth there. Instead she went down my leg oh under the knees

yellow

nipping my toes teeth sharp as a cat's then licking my thighs oh my belly my flat nipples oh her tongue sharp on my nipples the between-my-legs part is burning aching hot but it feels good how can anything that sharp feel good? under my arms and down my arms "Yer s'pose to purr" she says I have been holding my breath obediently I purr between short gasps wanting her to touch between my legs more than ever and wondering at my wish. She turns me over licking and biting along my shoulders and neck purring or growling at me occasionally is this still a game? I cannot bear it and I want her to never stop, her licking at the lower curve of my ass I biting my lip and holding my breath again feeling like I'm about to turn into air or steam. Turning over, "Annie . . ." she shushes me kissing my thighs again she is kissing not licking then she is cautiously pushing my trembling thighs apart looking up into my eyes, "D'ye want to play?" her eyes question see the answer in mine then her tongue touching me and I moan she stops, "Did that hurt?" "No" I whisper "please . . ." her tongue touching me again caressing that wrinkle of flesh at the center of my cleft. It does hurt and I feel some deep opening, some emptiness that never felt empty before. Then something happens and I dissolve in wetness tears flowing out of my eyes. I come back to myself clutching her shoulders she lying on top of me propped up on her forearms, looking searchingly into my damp gaze. "Are ye alreet?" I'm not sure what I am but I nod and smile. "Good." Annie huffs down beside me. "Then 'tis my turn to be the kitten and ye be the mumcat."

I soon discovered that I could make Annie melt like she had made me. Her body got very tense as I licked her and for a while I thought she was wroth with me 'cause when I reminded her to keep purrin' she said "Not now!" in a harsh voice. But then she grabbed my hair and pressed my face deeper into her cleft and cried out. I tasted smoke salt flowers and again dissolved.

Later we kissed and solemnly swore to keep our new

knowledge a secret. But Annie and I did not know the meaning of the word discretion. Oh, we did not actually talk to anyone about it, and at first probably no one suspected. But as we grew older other villagers began to narrow their eyes at us running down the street holding hands or sauntering in the smithy or at the Inn with our arms around each other.

One day at the smithy watching John Herrick at his trade. Sean, the Laird's son, watching wistfully the smith's skill for he longed to make things with his hands. Several other village men lounging near the forge drinking whisky for comfort against the cold winds. Annie and I with our cloaks around each other clinging together for warmth, the smokey smell of her hair in my nostrils. The men called for us to come sit in their laps share their whisky and get warm. Their laughter is hearty, the lewdness of their interest obvious. I'm no insulted but I'm no tempted neither. Annie feels too good to move. "We're fine as we are," I call back. "Yer too old tae be clinging tae each other like snotty-nosed bairns," one joshes. "An' too smart tae be clinging tae the likes of you," retorts Annie, kissing me full on the mouth in front of them. We toss our hair like wild horses and canter off through the snow, laughing at the looks on their faces. But while I laugh I feel a cold hard knot in my middle, a fear that someday these men will remember us playing them for fools, and pay us back for it.

yellow

CALIFORNIA RAINMAN

■

*Arlene
Stone*

The hairs on her neck his breath is blowing   hair soft as
a duck's behind   the curve of the neck's Doric column   the
fluting   His head that gleams like St Peter's dome

Svengali   *Bald heads are best*

Her legs his threshold   rain licking her leaves soft-spoken
moonlight   the olive trees whipped with rain whips
to green's primeval sheen   and winter camellias
ripen fall and fold   lingerie discarded   to rust in rain like
petals in a bowl   the eucalyptus long-waisted maidens stripped
by rain   their satin-handed lover   the mustard pungent as
Lethean ovens   fields hammered by rain to Grecian gold   the
rain putting out for a moment   the orangeries lit globes

Sven Rainman a collage   his face wallpapers peeling to gardens
he has trod   Rose/Gardenia/Camellia

She loves me   She loves me not

The one with milky thighs   Capri the garden in the perfumed
evenings   the tile floors cold as Campari on ice
Dawn bursts with bougainvillea reds   anisette after-births
& bitter lemon curd   the garbage man beating the sidewalks
with dropped lids

She loves me   she loves me not

SILK

The touch of knees under the table   The half-averted glances
torrid as blood oranges cut open   The murmured moments incom-
plete as rain beads on a branch   transient as light's passage
on a sky tongue-tied with thunder   & lightning messages ob-
scure as codices from Cretan tombs

Svengali Rainman   world voyeur on Mastersplurge   cruises
the nubile Napa valley   his features hard
to fix as stone the rain has rubbed for eons   his face a
rubbing   a man in the moon that took a million years
to form   the scar across his lip incised with stars

On her back helpless as an insect   hearing   for the third
month rain on rain   cat on her belly   the hearts four sea
sons split into rainy quadrants   plays with her belly cotton

He loves me   He loves me not
He loves me   He loves me not

His hand that is rain probes the tip of her iceberg tit
Sven the Arctic Admiral feeling his periscope at the North
Pole   flirts with a pretty Eskimo   warming her   seal beard
with his laprobe   circling the pink bud oh yes circling
yes as the taut bud opens yes and yes   the skin velvet
flocked   sundots blazing the eyes yes oh yes paint the
walls a cyclamen pink   paint her hot   paint her pinko and
faster and hotter yes yes   oh yes yes hotter than hashish

Rain   darling

Sven Rainman's rain drum drumming

Thunder under her mountain oh yes

"I'm NOT WHAT

YOU THOUGHT"

THE RAVISHER

■

Charles Semones

for D.D.

I'm not what you think:

My fingers do things
you would not believe.
My tongue goes crazy
in the dead of night.

I'm no chaste poet,
no celibate saint.

I'm not what you thought:

Rootbruised and moody,
I roil the bedclothes,
dream you in the nude.

I'd touch your body
to my body, strike
pentecostal flames.

I'm no dry eunuch,
no earthstunned angel.

I'm not what you hoped:

I baffle the eaves
with low syllables
you may wake up to,
go by all day long.

I make siege of wind,
ravishment by fire:
with me, you might be
loveseized inside out.

I'm no tame bedmate,
no easy savior.

I'm not what you know. . . .

Yellow

DANCING WITH
LUCHA

■

Geoffrey Fox

Héctor wanted to think about politics, but all he could think about was that girl. *La lucha* and La Lucha, the struggle and her. He tried to focus on the first but the other kept popping up.

It wasn't just the name, which was common enough. But he seemed to be unable to avoid her, especially since he had to spend so much time over by her house talking to her brother. And Remigio was a good candidate for the Party, really.

What would it be like to hold that hip? Just for a moment, to see if it would hold still.

And then, when they were alone a minute, inside her *rancho* with its smell of damp rotting cardboard, and casually, as though it wasn't really important, he asked if maybe she'd like to visit some friends on Friday night and listen to some records and expecting her to say she couldn't, or that she'd have to ask her father or her brother, or that she didn't do that kind of thing.

And she had puckered her black eyebrows into a frown, nodded her head with her lips bunched forward, and said, with rising inflection, "*Bueno,*" and grinned.

What kind of a girl was that, who would say "yes" just like that?

Maybe she wasn't really afraid of Remigio at all and just did what she pleased, at least when he wasn't around. Her father didn't seem to care what she did, so if she didn't obey her brother Remigio, who would she obey? Ah, women! At bottom, they couldn't be trusted. They always wanted to be independent. But sometimes, like with this one, that's what made them appealing.

Well, in a way it was better this way, her deciding on her own. He didn't want to feel under any *obligation* to her brother. So far it had been the other way, Remi deferred to him, sought

SILK

him out, and that was good. It was good politically. He'd make a good cadre, Remigio. But if they started mixing other things into the relationship, there would be problems, it would be confusing, undisciplined.

And there was this girl, the non-political Lucha, the one of flesh and bone, with cinnamon-color skin and laughing brown eyes and the most expressive rich brown lips—it was her mouth, the white smile, the quick pucker, the way the lips curled up as though to suck or laugh or do both at once, it was that wonderful mouth that came to mind most often. Even her hair was pretty in a way, stiff and black like his own but even curlier. Bad hair, *pelo malo*, really, African hair, but he didn't mind. And, he thought, he needed a girl, even a revolutionary needs a *jeva* of his own. As long as she's not too independent.

And she had said "*Bueno,*" with that big smile.

Just like that.

Now he sat on the stiff green plastic covering of one of Nélida's chairs and shuffled his feet against the polished concrete floor, a glass of rum in his hand, and only half-listened as Nélida told Lucha about her youth in Bogotá. Lucha was wearing a white party dress and though her head was bent down shyly, she was smiling.

He looked around the familiar room in this, one of the best-made cardboard *ranchos* in the *barrio*. Its panels of *cartón piedra* were tacked to the uprights both inside and outside, making two smooth surfaces that were painted blue outside and pale green, to match the furniture inside. He admired that neat attention to detail. There were no religious images on the walls, not even a calendar, which had seemed odd to him the first time he visited, since in other ways the room resembled his mother's parlor. Instead, there were some framed full-color magazine pictures: an Indian shepherd and his flock in the Andes, a reproduction of a painting of Bolivar at the battle of Araure, and a portrait of a wild-looking bearded man that

yellow

Tomás had said was Dostoyevsky. On top of the radio-phonograph case was a tinted photo that must have been Nélida as a teenager, with three other girls, and a black-and-white photograph of a young Tomás, with mustache and wearing a dark suit. The position of his shoulder suggested that his arm had been around somebody, but the photo had been cropped.

Tomás today was probably close to forty. He was still and somber whereas Nélida was quick and bird-like. His long hands hardly moved when he talked, except to light one cigarette after another and to carry them to and from his mouth. His only other gestures were with those large, serious dark eyes and an occasional inclination of the head, and this made him seem more serious. He was tall and thin and white, with a hawk nose and wavy black hair and a very heavy black shadow that threatened to blossom into a beard if he relaxed his vigilance. To Héctor he looked like a Spaniard. Though originally from Caracas, he had been on Communist Party business in Bogotá when he met Nélida. He had been doing something for, or maybe it was against, Gaitán just before he was murdered, and he had been in the Bogotazo riots and been deported, or escaped, none of this was clear from his laconic references, and had come home to Venezuela. He'd left Nélida behind then, but she'd found him again, years later. Héctor didn't ask for details, there were always embarrassing things in the past that it was better to respect. And of course there was no need for Lucha to know any of this.

Lucha was telling Nélida that she had got as far as fourth grade ("Just like me," Nélida said), that she didn't much care for housework or cooking but she liked caring for her little brother, Benjamín, whom she'd left tonight with Gladys, Remigio's girlfriend (Héctor hadn't known that Remi had a girlfriend in the *barrio*—but this meant someone else knew that Lucha and he were together, that even Remigio would know if he didn't already), that she liked to read about other countries.

SILK

"Let's put on some music," he suggested. Let's make this festive, let's *do* something. He could hear the boleros and announcements from the neighbors' radios.

Tomás got up somberly and examined his small, prized collection of records. He found a cumbia, "in honor of Nélida," he said.

His *companera* rose and invited Lucha, by gesture, to dance.

Nélida was the shorter, quicker and more comical in her movements of the two. Her young partner, warmed by the attention, turned pert and aggressive. She knew how to dance the cumbia, too, and she picked up and imitated the inventions in her partner's footwork. The two men watched and sipped their drinks as trumpets and cornets blared into their ears and, at their eye-level, hips thrust and swerved in time to the fast music.

Another record dropped, sounding the first soft strains of another bolero. Lucha stepped over to Tomás and pulled at his hand.

"Oh, no," laughed Nélida, "Tomás doesn't dance!"

But Lucha insisted, and soon the tall pale figure was standing erect, a cigarette still in his fingers, looking awkward and shy, a way that Héctor had never seen him, and stiffly held the girl as she pulled him into the first steps of the slow melodrama of a bolero. Dee dee dee *dee*-dee, da da da *da*-da, dee da da daaa, etc.

Héctor's smile froze as he watched. He didn't know what he felt, but he was being forced to do something. So he bounced to his feet—he could feel the rum in his throat—and grasped little Nélida—he'd never held her or even touched more than her hand before. He would show her, and Lucha too if she cared to watch, how a *venezolano* dances a bolero.

"Ooh," Nélida gave a little gasp of applause as he, eyes half closed, released her and rotated in a slow rhythmic spin, before returning to twirl her.

Another record dropped. One Héctor knew.

Yellow

La brisa tropical, a orilla de la mar . . ." and then

> Da-da-*da* da-da-*da* da-*da*-da,
> da-*da*-da, *da*-da da-da *da* da
> *El sabor de tu boca fresca, me oye,*
> *vale más qu'una joya.*
> *El calor que te da le arena comparo*
> *sólo con la gloria.*

And he was dancing with Lucha. He didn't notice when Tomás and Nélida stopped dancing, he just kept on, holding her close during the boleros, twirling and maneuvering her vigorously during the fast numbers, releasing her reluctantly when she wanted to step away to dance her own patterns. Hours later, he was warmer and rasher, he had at last been dancing with Lucha, it had been a contest it seemed, she was determined to keep up with his fancy steps and to introduce her own. Then, in the boleros, they danced slowly and he pressed her body against his, and she didn't resist. But it was getting late, it was time to do something, something else, to leave Tomás and Nélida's place and to move on to the next plane.

After a brief conference with Tomás, he stepped out into the cool, noisy night of a Friday in the *barrio*, to drag Otto from a domino game, and soon Lucha, protesting but also laughing, was stumbling alongside him as he pulled her to Otto's Chevrolet and Otto, sworn to secrecy, drove out of the dusty *barrio* and toward the city.

He left them at a bar with a jukebox and bright colored lights. More rum, with Pepsi for the lady. (*La dama! No jodas,* he thought.) Héctor dropped a coin into the Rock-ola.

The blast of trumpets only momentarily startled the other couples, who went back to their drinks and their embraces in the dark booths.

SILK

La brisa tropical
    The tropical breeze
      a orilla de la mar
        at the edge of the sea

le da un rico sabor
    gives a sweet taste
      a tu boquita
        to your mouth,
            your sweet little mouth.

Debajo del palmar
al sol de tu mirar
Permíteme sonar
en tu boquita

Beneath the palms
by the sun of your gaze
Let me dream
of your sweet mouth

". . . *en tu boquita*," he murmured into her ear, "*la estrene de la sal/da un sabor sensual/que invita a saborear tu boquita.*"

    He wanted more rum, but he also wanted to kiss that *boquita*, he wanted to *disfrutar/el más dulce placer/besando sin cesar* to enjoy the sweetest pleasure, to kiss and kiss without ceasing *tu boquita* those full brown lips. She struggled. "*Lucha, no luches,*" he murmured, she laughed but still tried to turn her face from his. At last the mouth was against his mouth, the lips pressing, pulling, fighting with his lips. He imagined it tasted salty, that mouth, like in the song, but it didn't, it was just hot and tasted a little like warm milk and mush. Her hands and arms, which had been pushing him away, now grabbed his shoulders and pulled him toward her, or so he made himself believe.

    And then they were in a room in the back, a room so airless he had to work to haul in oxygen full of mildew and other people's sweat but it didn't matter, because soon he had her

yellow

clothes off and his fingers around her nipple, so soft and rubbery he felt a flash of guilt or rather annoyance that she was more frightened than excited. Trying to drive her up to his wild heat, he forced his mouth against her mouth and his other hand under the smooth, small back, resisting while her hand pressed hard against his chest until, in a sudden change of course, he felt that hand slip down and tug twice at his belt and the nipple stiffened, quivering and eager, and he sheathed his teeth with his lips to nip and suck on that nipple that was still growing now in his mouth and now at last he tasted the salt of the song and he smelled something from her that he imagined to be the sea-brine *a orilla de la mar* and he heard his pants clump to the floor *la brisa tropical* while with his thumb he traced the line of her thigh *el más dulce placer* inward to the crisp curled hairs *de tu boquita*. Her small body shuddered *sin cesar* and clung *permíteme sonar* to him and all of his awareness surged into an enormous swollen pulsing that poked and probed *en tu boquita*, until at last *un sabor sensual* he pierced and nestled in her moist desiring fear *besando sin cesar* deep deep inside her *boquita*.

II

(Héctor has been arrested by the government police, and, after being severely beaten and electroshocked, is finally released from prison.)

Héctor didn't have a watch anymore—the Digepol had stolen it—but the sun told him it was close to three as he rushed to his appointment. He was surprised when his feet hit concrete, because he had forgotten about the new stairs. Well, he could look at them later, at first glance they seemed better than anything he could have expected from his brother-in-law, and they made the descent much faster, especially when you were bounding, two or three steps at a time.

His momentum almost carried him into the stream, but his old baseball practice saved him as he twisted back in the air to land just on the edge. He looked around, but didn't see Lucha. Two women he scarcely knew, their skirts rolled above their knees as they stood in the water, looked up at him with scowls.

"Good day," he said, as pleasantly as he could. He was out of breath.

"Good day," they grunted back, and returned to their washing, but continued to peer at him over their shoulders. He realized he had invaded women's territory and wanted to retreat, but he was supposed to meet Lucha here. He was pretending to be jaunty and at ease, but the result was that his body and head just sort of wiggled as he stood there, first on one leg, then on the other. *Mierda*, where was she? The women were watching him as though he were crazy.

He heard a whistle and turned. So did the two women in the stream, of course. Lucha was a little farther upstream, holding back the full green leaves of a large plantain plant.

"*Bueno, adiós.*"

Héctor nodded pleasantly to the women, who just stared at him as he walked quickly toward Lucha. Before he reached her, she turned and continued farther upstream. He followed as swiftly as he could, but she was faster, as though she knew this territory and its underbrush intimately. When at last she let him catch up to her, they were around a bend and out of sight of the washing women. Because of the contours of the land and the thickness of the wild plantains and bananas and other plants, they were out of sight of all the *ranchos* except one isolated cabin of *bahareque*, which had no opening cut through its mud walls on the side facing them.

She turned and sat abruptly in a spot where the grass had already been crushed to her exact dimensions.

"Well?" she said, looking up at him.

She was beautiful in that dappled light, filtered through the plantain, more beautiful than ever because of the strangeness of this place, made stranger yet by being so close to the dense and

YELLOW

busy *barrio* but screened from it. Perhaps if he had come to the *barrio* as a child he would have discovered this spot, but he hadn't and neither had any other man he knew. He thought of enchanted forests from his boyhood fairy tales, and even more he thought of his own secret hiding places from that time. He had tracked the enchantress to her *guarida*, her lair.

"You're beautiful!" he said.

"Don't talk nonsense!"

The answer was curt, but he thought she looked pleased.

"Really, you are. It's not nonsense."

"Don't come to me with your flowers, plucked from another's garden," she sang.

"No, really, these aren't 'flowers,' I mean it truly. You are lovely, the most lovely thing I have ever seen!"

"I am a poor *negrita* whose heart you think you can play with, and then, when you return, you already have forgotten."

"You're no blacker than I am. In fact, I think you're a little lighter. Look."

He moved to put his arm up against hers but she withdrew her arm and her shoulder.

"I'm not talking about color, *bobo*."

He knew that. He just wanted to feel his skin against hers. And she knew that, too. He made a place for himself in the grass next to her. She shifted away, but only slightly. It was a game, like her running ahead of him had been, he thought.

"Three days you've been back! Mati told me."

"Well, I had to rest. I wasn't feeling very well when I, when I got out of there."

She turned to him now, worried. "Did they hurt you?"

"Oh, well, nothing special."

He was glad for the sympathy, but at the same time he couldn't exploit it, because he didn't want to talk about what had happened.

"What did they do? Tell me."

He made a sad-funny frown and waved his hand, as though shooing flies.

Her face still looked caring and concerned, but she hardened her eyes a little and said, "Well, it doesn't matter. You could have sent me word, even if you didn't feel like walking all the way to my house." All thirty meters, she meant.

He let his lip quiver a little. Perhaps it would be all right to show some emotion other than joy around this girl. Perhaps it would make her relent so that she would let him touch her again. But not too much emotion.

"*Morrocoy*, tell me what they did to you," she said, grasping him by the shoulders so that he had to face her.

He looked up, surprised.

"Who told you about that nickname?"

"*You* did, *bobo*. You don't even remember. I'll bet you don't remember half the things you said that night!"

There were tears in her eyes. This surprised him, too. He lost track of who was supposed to be comforting whom.

"No, I told you that? Sure, I remember, I remember everything that night, but I don't remember telling you about that nickname. That's from when I was a baby."

He relaxed a little, taking the initiative as the comfortee, and she cradled him.

"You were my baby that night," she said, "like now. My little baby."

He laughed, but made no attempt to escape her arms.

"I was afraid you didn't respect me," she said, "that you thought I was too easy."

"No, my love. How could I not respect you?"

"Lots of boys are like that. They want a girl to go to bed, and then they don't respect her."

"I'm not like that."

And as he said it, he thought, *I wasn't the first*.

"What's the matter?" she asked, and he realized that he had

yellow

stiffened involuntarily. He pulled back a little, but still in her arms, and looked up at her puzzled face.

"I wasn't the first, was I?"

She released him and stared at him with a terrible look, as though she had just seen something ugly and frightening. Then she turned her face away. He waited for a response, but suddenly she started to get up. He grabbed her arm and held her down.

"Let me go!"

"Lucha, don't go, my love. Please."

She pulled but he held firm. She turned away from him. Her head and neck trembled.

"You men are so cruel. The first! That's all you care about, being first! Did I ask you that question?"

He stopped. He stopped everything, though still holding her arm. Such a thought! Unheard of! Or nearly so—he remembered a debate between Lenin and a crazy Russian woman, who said that it should matter no more for the woman than for the man. But this ignorant girl could know nothing of that.

"Lucha, it's not the same."

"Why not?"

"I'm a man."

She looked at him fiercely. What he was supposed to do, what most of the men he knew would do, was to slap her, beat her if necessary, until he beat the insolence out of her. He had seen this, it was the virile thing to do.

But then, he had made another commitment, he was a Communist, he was supposed to have answers or, if he had no answers, he was supposed to try to reason scientifically. And besides, he had let the moment pass.

"I don't know," he said.

He released her arm.

"You don't love me. For you, I was just another conquest. And when it is inconvenient or you're bored, you don't think of me."

Her eyes were dry now, her voice hard.

He winced.

"No, *Luchita*, my love," he began, trying to persuade them both, "I do love you. And I'm sorry I asked that question. It was a stupid thing. Forgive me. All those days I was in prison, I kept thinking of you. And not just the part about being in bed, although that was wonderful to remember too, but your laugh and your beautiful eyes. I even love your hair."

"Bad hair."

"I don't care. I love it. It's like mine. I don't think I told you this, but one reason they call me *Gallito* is because of my hair, it's so stiff it stands up in front like a crest."

"It's all right for a man to have that kind of hair."

"Hey, what are you saying? You were the one who was telling me things should be the same for a man and a woman, right? I like your hair. And I like you."

He was holding her now, her head nestling against his chest. He was amazed at the effect of his own performance. And yet it wasn't only a performance, he meant these things, too. Didn't he? This wasn't the kind of hair he dreamed about when he fantasized about girls, but those were just empty fantasies, Lucha was a real person, and she came all together, you couldn't have that wonderful mouth without also having this hair and those beautiful eyes and those high, round little breasts that now were pressing against his midriff and that insolence that you could see even in her walk and that he'd seen just now in the fieriness of her retort, and he wanted her all, and everything about her then was beautiful.

They murmured to each other, she tensed as his hand moved toward her breast, then she relaxed and opened her bosom to him. He palpated its roundness, found the stiffening nipple through the cloth, felt her smaller hand at his waist, moving up and down his ribs, around to the small of his back, they wriggled until the grasses had ceded a bed to them, he re-

Yellow

moved his hand and reached under the skirt and up her trembling thigh, sliding past the cotton briefs protecting her sex, on up under the dress to her nipple, slipping the breast free of the small brassiere, squeezing the breast gently, pulling, rotating the stiff resilient nipple, her hips moved, rocked, her pelvis pressed against him, he kissed her open mouth and tasted her tongue, which jumped back from his at first but then returned and sought his eagerly. Her free hand tugged at the waistband of his pants. He winced as the hand on his back touched a recent bruise, but it didn't matter. He helped her open his pants, he rolled back on his side as she pulled out his hard penis, she looked at it as his hand now played over the soft brown curve of her hip, she pushed back the dark foreskin and pulsated the penis, up and down, steadily, slowly, he pulled down her white briefs—they had never seen each other, these parts of each other, in the daylight before—and he played in the crisp curls of her pubis, then probed the moist fleshiness inside with his index finger and her hips gyrated more and she closed her eyes and leaned her head back, her mouth open, her arm still stretched out with her hand firmly on his stiff member. The iron-green smell of the plants now ceded to her musk. His nostrils flared. Then at last he rolled back on top of her and she guided him inside her and he kissed her long and deep and moved slowly, powerfully, bringing her, bringing her, bringing her to spasms until at last he too let go, and shook, and then relaxed, collapsing in her grasp.

They lay there afterward, side by side, in the shadows of the foliage, his hand on her flat smooth belly and her slender hand on his.

"Am I your woman, then?"

"Of course you are! My woman. My *Luchita*. And I'm your man."

" '*Gallito*,' '*Morrocoy*,' such funny animal names! I think I'll call you '*Tigre*.' "

He grinned and looked at her.

"Then we're of the same species," he said.

"Do you love me?"

"You know I do."

"More than anything?"

"More than anything!"

He wondered if he were telling the truth.

"Little tiger," she said, "why didn't you come to me when you were hurt.?"

He answered with a comic growl and hid his face between her breasts.

yellow

HOW ALIENS SURVIVE ON THIS PLANET (WHY MOTHER AND I GARDEN)
■

Bonnie Roberts

Mother was a beautiful earthling,
planting on the farm
and the green alien came in a silver ship and
looked down upon her and spread his martian seed
in the tube rose, mint and wild grape of evening air.
She walked the furrows laughing,
and wet her toes in the back door faucet,
and thus conceived me,
mud and water body, alien soul.
Sometimes we long for my father to return in his ship
and search for him in the whirling orbs of the spring sky
and Mother and I, by the moon, plant tomatoes,
    potatoes and peas,
harvesting more and more green each summer,
signaling.

SILK

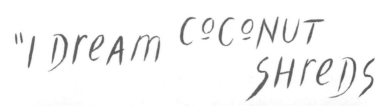

"I DREAM COCONUT SHREDS

FALL INTO HOT MILK"

MY LOVEMAKING IS AUTOBIOGRAPHICAL

■

Bonnie Roberts

With my hands, I draw my memories on his body.
The red hibiscus pollen on his cheek,
the creaking rope swing on his belly,
the August Ferris wheel on his groin.
My paints are soft and thick like the dust from Nate's Lane
and the layer of fall leaves on the front porch
   of the haunted house.
I even spread some between his toes.
And he sees my mother and father and sister
sitting down to dinner at the green oak table
and, after the dishes are done, me, standing on the little chair,
washing my long hair over the round sink,
stroking all the suds to the ends
and blowing them from my hands
and the towel around my neck and the sleeves
   of my muslin gown,
rimmed in wetness.

yellow

TEA WITH RITA

■

*Sarah
Randolph*

Of the hour we had to clean before she arrived we spent
  forty-five
minutes making love. When she comes in we are breathless
  and swept,
even the kettle steaming. Ginger biscuits and shortbread
  from friends

already across the country. I pour. My lover and she choose
  regularly
the medium of family news for their communication,
  which pleases me,
like a hearth, to sit by. I sit by. I dream coconut shreds fall
  into hot milk.

Brooklyn, Iowa City, a mother-in-law from Greece
  unexpectedly comfortable
with the breakfast dishes. I fall into white sheets, books fall
  off the bed;
fall apart, fall open, fall in. My own relatives enter the story
  eating turkey;

unrelentingly blond, they refrain from inquiring
  into the meaning of my
lover's presence. Her family says fuck, mine does not.
  My family's native
indifference or tact keeps us virtually silent. I watch
  a few missed books

under the couch, her feet do not touch them. Soft dustclouds.
   A saucer of oil
on the bedside table. I do not know what she sees
   as she stands back
for a Polaroid photograph of the two lovers. We look
   at ourselves

as we did in the presence of our relations, slightly overexposed
   but happy.
She leaves us with this and an hour later we are back
   on the bed eating,
this time shrimp poached in coconut milk and fresh herbs.

yellow

JEWEL OF
THE MOON

■

*William
Kotzwinkle*

She and Mother watched through the curtains as the handsome stranger and Father discussed her marriage. The stranger offered money, which Father said was too little. Then they smoked and Father grew poetic, calling her Jewel of the Moon, and she was afraid the bargaining would never finish. She desperately hoped it would, for the stranger was fine-looking and the frog-faced rug-seller of the village was also seeking her hand. Take me away, whispered her heart, and perhaps the stranger felt its delicate beat, for he suddenly doubled his offer of gold and Father agreed.

On the day of their marriage a celebration was held in the village. The drums spoke their hollow song, she danced, the sun was bright. Then as afternoon grew late, he took her away, onto the country road, toward his own village.

Confused, frightened, delighted, mad with anxiety, a virgin, she did not know what to say to him, though her thighs spoke silken words through her gown as she walked along the dirt road, aflame.

The setting sun cast her husband's face in deep red. His eyes burned through her and she too grew red, her stomach flip-flopping, young and silly, but her breasts were moving sweetly as she walked, her hips were full and swayed and how pretty were her bare painted toes. Her ears dangled with earrings and through their jingling she heard the sound of a distant flute.

"That is the musician of my village, welcoming you," said her husband.

She fell into sadness. To strange music, into a strange town, with childhood gone, Jewel of the Moon is letting herself be led. But circling, dancing in the air, the song enticed her, set her dreaming. Soon she would let her black hair down.

Ahead she saw the trees and rooftops of his village, and doubt ruined her again. Afraid to look at him now, she pulled

SILK

her veil over her head, to hide, to die. How cruel of Father to abandon her, to trade Jewel of the Moon for two bags of gold to this stranger.

"Here we are," he said, turning onto a narrow dirt path.

At the end of the path she saw a small house. Slowly she walked toward it, numb with fear. Still she kept dignity, which Mother had taught her to maintain always, whatever the situation. She did not slouch, tremble, or faint crossing the strange threshold to the cool gloom of the living room. Out of the corner of her eye, through a small doorway, she saw the rattan foot of a bed.

Her husband pointed toward that room and she walked to the doorway, heart thundering.

A purple lamp hung there, and her skin turned to pale moon shades as she walked through the opening. My husband is an exotic, she thought, inspecting the ornate shade of the lamp, on which a thousand-armed God was embracing his naked purple-skinned wife. Will I be sophisticated or will I scream? In the purple den of love, she turned to face him.

He unwrapped the white marriage turban from his head and dark hair fell to his shoulders. Tenderness? Or will he ravish me with bloody sword? Her body played possibilities as he lit incense on the tiny altar by the bed.

She looked down at her toes, wanting to conceal the rest of herself from him, wanting also to reveal what he hadn't seen, wanting this and wanting that, frozen flame in a purple place. The window was near and she could escape, but she longed to surprise him with the fullness of her thighs.

"Sit down," he said. She sat on the edge of the bed, dropping her hips into the soft embrace of the mattress. I am ready.

He knelt before her, looked into her eyes. This is the moment.

"I'll sleep down here," he said, stretching himself out on the floor at her feet.

I must awake, she thought, trying to escape the silly dream.

yellow

"Perhaps you would like a glass of milk with a piece of toast?" he asked, raising himself on one elbow.

She looked dumbly at the far wall of the bedroom, as her husband hustled off to the kitchen. Nervously, she opened the ribbon on her hair and let her long black head-cloak fall scented and shimmering. I am Jewel of the Moon. Why does he talk of milk and toast?

"Here I am," he said, coming toward her on his knees, holding the milk and toast.

She took the plate. He turned back down at her feet. "Just kick me if you want anything else."

I have married a madman. Jewel of the Moon peered over the edge of the bed.

Her husband's eyes quickly opened. "Anything else, Perfect One?"

Unable to speak, she shook her head, and though she was not hungry she ate the toast. Then she stretched out on the wedding bed and stared at the ceiling. I must escape. She waited until she was sure he was asleep, but as soon as her foot touched the floor, he was up, like a watchdog, watching her.

Frightened, she lay back down. She would look for another chance, but sleep overtook her, and she spent the night dreaming of a powerful horse who galloped her to freedom.

"Here is your breakfast, Daughter of the Sun," said her ridiculous husband in the morning, coming toward her on his knees with a silver tray of food.

She ate and he sat at her feet, watching the window, heedless of her morning beauty, as if his fearful bargaining for her had never been. She was truly miserable, for it was real, had been no dream, she'd married an imbecile. That is what he looks like, sitting there. He looks like an incredible idiot and I hate him.

"Here," she said, contemptuously, "I'm done."

"At once." Taking away her cup and plate, he scurried off

to the kitchen. She watched him return, to the doorway only, where he lay down, and she covered her tearful eyes. Peeking through her fingers, she saw him lying there, doglike, eyes on her, bright, stupid. She wanted to wave her tail at him, give him something to growl about.

"I'm going for a walk," she said, defiantly stepping over the crumpled man on the floor. Perhaps he will bite me, seek to hold me somehow.

"I'll just walk a few paces behind you," he said. "If you want anything, just spit on me."

They walked through the streets of his strange village. She knew no one there, except the shadowy dog at her heels. He lapped along behind her to the well. Women were fetching water and they gave her inquiring looks, as her husband curled up at her feet in the sand. They know I've been tricked by a weak-kneed fiend. Looking down, she wanted to spit on him, but the women would love that too much.

She left the well and walked on through the village, curling her toes in the hot sand as the men of this new village eyed her bare feet and a bit more, perhaps, for her hips were expressing themselves, too enthusiastically for a married woman, but her so-called husband was licking along at the ground. I'll give him one more chance this afternoon.

She sat upon the bed, brushing her long hair over her heart. Her ankles were smooth and bare and she wriggled her toes as he entered the room, bathed in the gold of afternoon. But there came no spicy kiss upon her toes, only curried peas, served on a tray which he placed on her thighs.

Night. Beneath purple light he gave her milk and toast and curled down again on the floor. The milk and toast made her brain sleepy, but her pale thighs wanted something indescribably nice, and it wasn't milk toast.

She tossed on her pillow, recalling the passages from the Holy Sutra on Love. I studied the book faithfully, yet here I

yellow

am, perspiring on an empty bed. She rose up and with her bare foot gave her husband a kick.

He rolled over, looking up from the floor like a whipped mongrel.

"Stop snoring," she said, angrily.

"I will stop breathing," he said, and wrapped a strip of linen around his nose.

The moon crossed her pillow. Slowly her passion subsided, like a body fallen away, and she moved in dreams, a queen with many servants, all of them her idiot husband.

As the wedding month went by, she grew tense. Her husband was silent, devoted, treated her like a queen, and she loathed him and his entire line of ancestors. She thrust her foot out, so that he might remove her sandals, which he did, handling her foot as carefully as a dish of precious rice, except that he did not taste or swallow the delight and it soon grew cold.

She raised her feet on the barren marriage bed, drawing her knees up to her breasts. I am so young. There are other men. They would not treat me like this. They would torture me with glances, drive me mad with their eyes. I will die soon of dullness. Neglect can end woman's life, so says the Holy Sutra.

She felt the end of the mattress suddenly sink down with unusual force. "What are you doing?" she cried, for the impudent servant was sitting on the foot of the bed.

"If you want anything," he said, curling up at her feet, "just kick me in the face."

She pulled herself into a fetal ball, wishing she could be reborn in some hidden world. The night bird blew his flute, she lay in purple moon-robe, and dreams of mating came to her. A shining man held her, ghostly thin he was, and she stretched herself out beneath him, at the same time touching with her toe accidentally the face of the vile sleeper at her feet.

"Yes, Tower of Grace," said her husband, sitting up quickly, "have you bad dreams? I will make a cup of tea which relaxes the mind."

He left and returned with a silver tray, surrounded by steam. He poured the tea and she let the sheet fall away from her, moonlight coming on her breasts, bare behind her thin midnight gown.

"This will help," he said, handing her a cup of the tea, not even glancing at the pale cups she had so immodestly revealed. She drew the sheet around herself again, hating him, and drank the tea, a gentle herb, which soon brought the charm of sleep.

Each night, following milk and toast, he slipped onto the foot of the bed, like a dog trained to warm the feet of his mistress. Silently, while he slept, she felt over his face lightly with her toe. The second month of their marriage passed this way, with her body inflamed by his nearness. Though his canine countenance expressed no more than a stupid smile, his simple animal nature inspired her, and in dreams she attacked him. *It has grown hot in this lagoon. I shall swim with him. She slipped into the warm water, where his silver face shined. Into his heat she swam.*

She woke, feverish. Her husband's hot breath was on her feet. Unable to resist, she tiptoed on the warm waves from his tongue, dancing there.

In the third month, the dog became a tortoise, crawling slowly up the mattress toward her. Each night she felt his shell coming closer. When she looked in the dark purple toward him, he seemed wrinkled as an ancient. His faithful dog-eye was gone and in its place was a wiser, if somewhat frightening beak, and two gleaming eyes, accustomed to the night sea.

She wanted to hide inside the pillow, to shrink into nothingness, to keep herself apart from his breathing on her knees, and from his devious turtle-eyes coldly haunting her.

Daytime brought her release from the illusion. She went to the temple and begged Kali to advise her. The beautiful altar goddess danced on the head of a slave. If only I could be fierce

yellow

as you, Goddess. The statue was mute. The distraught girl rose
and left the temple. Her husband was kneeling in the sand of
the temple garden, the sun upon his dark curling hair. If he
weren't so shifty, he might almost be good-looking, she
thought, walking slowly toward him.

That night he came slowly toward her, to her thighs with
his head. What fiendish ticklement is this, she wondered in a
moment of clarity, before the warm cream of his breath poured
over her thighs. She pressed them together to stop the sensation
and it grew more intense. She spread them apart trying to cool
them and her soft leg-flesh touched his nose.

"Yes, Queen," he said in a whisper.

"Please," she said, softly.

"What would you have me do?" asked the turtle.

Could she tell him her thighs were milk? She raised her
hips just a little.

"Is there a lump in the mattress, Gracious Saint?"

"Oh, the dog!" she cried and turned quickly away, but her
gown rose up so that perhaps he could see the soft underness of
her thighs. What an immodesty, she thought, quickly pulling
down her gown.

The fourth month of marriage brought the face of her husband directly in line with her secret. His breath upon her toes
had been inflaming; his breathing on her rose was driving her
insane. Streams of air reached between her thighs, gently handling her flower. She tried always to sleep on her stomach, so
she would not be subjected to warm southern winds, but in
dreams she soon rolled over again, into the tropic breeze from
his nose, which played over the hot little island between her
thighs.

Later, when they walked outside, she went head down,
deep in confusion. Caught in the rain, she made no attempt to
take cover. The cloudburst ran along her hot flesh and her hus-

band stood with her in the rain, and the village women no doubt thought them mad.

At five months, his face lay by her stomach. His breath blew her gown lightly; she touched him with her belly, upon his hooked nose.

His eagle-eye saw through her gown, to the soul in her rolling ocean of jelly, to the eye in her navel. Into that canyon of time went his nose, filling it with warmth. She lay perspiring like a holy woman on a bed of coals, though she did not feel holy, in fact, quite the opposite.

When six months ended, the wandering slave in her bed had lodged at her breasts. His eyes gleamed in the dark like an idol's. The purple light played on his face. She tried to cover her breasts, to hide them from his dark look, but they are so tender, they hurt me, let him look if he dares to. His breath touched her lightly on her soft little island tops, her red-peaked nipples. Excited as if she were dancing in the village, her breasts heaved and touched him. In the crevice of dreams where her heart lay concealed, she enclosed his nose.

It tickled ridiculously. That was its strange power. She was ten-thousand-times-over afraid of it, yet somehow withstood the invasion. Encircle his nose again, my breasts, smother him with your sweetness, drive him mad too.

He remained calm. Yet in the seventh month he was stretched out entirely beside her. Kinglike he slept, lightly, staring sometimes at the ceiling for long hours. Around her body was an envelope of heat, as if she were afloat in a warm cloud. His breath seemed to have lingered all over her body, gathering around it like a mist. His elbow touched her. Quickly she drew her arm away. This bed is far too small for two people. She withdrew to the farthest corner. But in curling up she bumped him with her backside and he, amazingly, returned the bump.

This shocking demonstration was repeated on the following

yellow

night and on many nights afterward. Like wandering taxis they bumped each other, bumper to bumper they lay pressed together in the street of feathers. It is mad play, but what pleasure. Later she rose up and looked at the impertinent fellow, naked to the waist in the moonlight.

"Yes, Lotus?" He woke and rose to her.

"I'm so thirsty," she said.

"At once," he said, and leapt out of the bed.

He returned with a cool drink of water. She drank it slowly and extended the glass back to him. As he retrieved it, his hand brushed light as a wing-tip across her breast. He put the glass down and crawled into bed beside her. Reaching for the thin sheet, the devil's finger touched her again. Her red breasts heaved to meet his hands, wanting that and wanting more.

On the following night, as he served her milk, she leaned in a most favorable angle and his palm touched underneath her breasts, in the softness, and lingered there.

Next night, she was seated on a cushion by the window. He came from the kitchen on his knees, bearing a tray on which a glass of red wine was balanced. He bowed. His black curling hair was like snakes in a dance. His hand came forward. All night he held the threads of her shoulder straps in his fingertips, and toward dawn he let them drop and half awake, half dreaming, she watched her left moon appear, naked, round, full.

Earlier, in the fashion of the slave girls, she had made herself up, reddening the nipple, tanning the round globe, even underneath, where the sun never came. Now, she dared not move, the silence was all around them. He stared at her breast like a devotee at a statue and she accepted his stare.

For days he stared at it, through the passing light of morning, afternoon, and evening. He pondered it from every angle, looking all around it and underneath it, like a monkey with a problem. She did not know what to do. Her thoughts were jumbled, her head was spinning, for they spent so much time in bed these days. Slowly his hand came forward. Was it an age or an instant that passed, she'd lost touch with time. Suddenly he was touching her on the left breast and fondling it.

So she spent the ninth month, one breast out. Each time she tried to tie her gown up, he untied it again. She felt so odd sitting eating dinner with one breast bare. Shortly after dinner he began stroking the other one, and each night it was the same, until the tenth month came and he slipped the knot on her right shoulder, rendering both breasts bare.

She sat, naked to the waist. All night he sat looking at her, and she at him. She nodded off to sleep finally, and her dreams were filled with insanity. She'd lost sight of father, mother, dignity, the world, except for two moons in the air. She felt a cloudy field all around her and she ran through a ghostly mist, awaking to his lips upon the tiny crater of her right moon.

Then he revolved both moons in his hands, until she was thrashing back and forth on the bed, most indecorously. She begged him to stop revolving them but he laughed and went on revolving them.

That morning she rose early and since she was in the kitchen before him, she prepared her own breakfast, and as an afterthought, prepared his too, and served it to him.

She knelt by the bed and slipped the tray over the covers. He opened his eyes and she lowered her own. He ate quietly and the sunlight came, turning the bed to a gold palanquin on which he seemed to float, looking down on her. She had covered her bosom to serve him. With a gesture of perfect sovereignty, he slipped the knots of her gown and bared her breasts again. He digested his breakfast, fondling them.

About noontime, after five hours of feeling her breasts, he began sucking them, first one, then the other, alternating on the hour. At dinnertime she could not help but scream, so tender had they grown from his feasting. This incredibly idiotic child is draining my soul, sucking it into himself, but she welcomed him nonetheless and in fact offered up to him with her hands the twin fruits.

yellow

By night he continued lowering her gown. Inch by inch he pulled it, a little each evening, until her stomach heaved up into the moonlight. Like a vast continent it came into view, but she did not feel continent, just the opposite, ravished as she was by feverish grindings in her stomach. He squeezed her moons and licked across the land of her belly, his moustache trailing in her navel.

Finally the gown was down to the edge of her secret. In a dream she was taken down the night to an ancient forest altar, a cave in which a priestess dwelled. It was a shimmering red crack in the mountain and she entered. The shining man was sitting on a throne, deep inside the cave.

She woke, moved her legs, felt suddenly free; her gown was gone. He was looking at her dark scented place, which sparkled as if with dewdrops. She felt older, parting her legs, then demurely closed them, feeling childish. He stared at it all night, and continued to stare at it throughout the morning, as the sun rose upon her little tangled grove. He ate lunch looking at it and spent the evening with his nose practically next to it. She felt herself burning alive.

She had to leave the bed. She ran naked through the house. He caught her in the kitchen, in a most peculiar position, putting his hand directly into her forest. She sank to her knees and bowed her head, worshipping him as he ran his finger all along the crack in the forest floor.

For the entire eleventh month he investigated that mysterious forest. He parted the underbrush so that the altar was plainly visible, and then like a blind man feeling letters, he ran his fingers along the sacred tabernacle, reading every wrinkle and fold. The altar streamed with the precious nectar. His finger slipped just the slightest bit inside it and remained there, all day, every day, for a month. She screamed, beating him about the head with her hands.

Silently, day by day, he worked like a hermit drawing with his finger on a cave wall. Then, by night, he brought his head to the cave and spoke a wordless whisper. She pressed her forest lips to his in silent answer and they kissed softly. All night, hour after hour, he kissed her there, while she squirmed, kicking her legs, beating her hands upon the mattress. For a month she writhed, groaning, in and out of delightful anguish.

From the devil he had learned to take in his lips the tiny turned-out root that hung from the mouth of her sacred cave. Known to no one, guarded and carefully hidden by her through all her years, it was now in the man's lips and he was humming on it. The tune was crazy, mad bees swarmed through her, but each time, just as she felt herself about to turn into sweetest honey, he stopped, leaving her hovering, dying, frantic.

They did not go out any longer. When he tried to lift his head away to bring food, she held him by the ears. The food grew cold and she grew hotter, running her fingers through his curly hair.

By day she followed him around the house, served him on her knees, washed his body, made his bed. He had enslaved her with his tongue. Her will was gone, sucked out in the night. Standing by the kitchen doorway, she moved aside to let him pass. His sleeping gown was loose and some devil played it open and she saw the outline of his manhood. He brushed past her and the hot organ touched her thigh.

Later in the day, as she bent over to pick up his slippers, he pressed it against her backside. Day after day then, she encountered it, and in her dreams she saw it standing on the throne inside the altar, shining, one-eyed, on fire.

Unable to resist any longer, she touched it, thinking he was asleep. He was not. He opened his eyes, fully awake.

"Please," she said. It was the twelfth month and she stretched out on the bed and spread her legs like a courtesan. Her forest stream was flowing, she was made of liquid, her body was undone, the veils of her passion unknotted.

"Please," she said, taking his member in her hand. He rose and knelt between her legs. Then he braced himself over her

yellow

and slowly, like a man falling in a dream, lowered himself.

The night fell upon her. His thighs rested on hers and against her altar she felt the hot hard pressing, not of a fist or a finger, but of a finer thing, a more distinguished tool, of shape divine, like the shining thing in her dreams, and she longed to take it into herself. She pressed her forest crack against the fleshy head, feeling its wet eyedrop. She nibbled with her clumsy forest lips, dumbly trying to swallow the burning Godhead.

Each night for a week it played at her melting doorway, and just when she thought she could stand its presence, it entered the buttery folds and she gasped with amazement for she could not stand it, so painful and terrible was it, at last. She gave her hips just the slightest move.

"Don't move," he said in a dark voice beside her ear, and she didn't.

They lay that way each night for a week, like trees fallen together in a storm. Her legs entangled his, locking at the ankles, and her tiny cave-root was engaged.

Pressing deeper each night, he soon reached the tiny red curtain across her virgin altar. He pressed harder, but the way was small, the pressure unbearable. The space is too tight, she thought, weeping. I can never fit this thing into me, it is unendurable, it . . . seems to be going in a little farther.

No longer a virgin, she howled, for the jewel of the moon was red with blood. The veil is burning, the veil is gone. God's body slipped slowly into her.

Wheels of flame revolved in her brain and in the forest cave the Godhead reigned, solemn, still, supreme, and she felt the beat of his burning heart-shape.

All night they lay that way, he did not allow her to move, but surreptitiously she managed to, flexing the tiny muscles of her secret mouth. Each time she did, lights appeared to her and her warm tears flowed. The dreams of mating danced round her, encircling her, and she was their center and her hair was entwined with his. There was a beat, it is slow, this coming of beauty, and their locked bodies brought it nearer, so that by dawn it had almost arrived.

The need for nourishment finally overtook them and that afternoon he withdrew the Godhead from her and her cave closed shut. This is reality, she thought, stumbling naked toward the kitchen. She fried them lunch, a festival of grains, and naked they ate, lightly.

At sundown she lay down again and parted her legs. We are on the mountain of pleasure. It goes into me again. I am reassured of its constancy. I am . . . quite full, dearest, come closer.

When it was fully lodged in her, she spread her legs in a wide V, and raising them into the air, kicked them about, laughing madly, with elephants dancing, serpents too, and she walked in her brain, room by room, through waking dreams, down the road of joy, tossing, turning, coming closer, to the mysterious presence. Panting, sweating, she held his buttocks, tried to make him move, to take them closer.

Not until the thirteenth month did he move, but that movement was definitive, marking a farther outpost of bliss. To feel his tool run in and out of me, that is the deep truth. Could there be more? She suspected another door.

Each night he stroked her once, so slowly, the entire night was needed for the length of his thousand-armed shaft to move in and out. At times she thought it was not moving at all, but it was, and in the extremities of slowness she saw concealed worlds.

Time changed; in a single second she saw great lengths of his organ. Breathless, afire, stupefied, she too learned to move slowly. Here the moment opens. In it are contained like tiny seeds a million more divisions. And she grew smaller.

It was the end of the thirteenth month. She loved him but wanted to reach their plateau, the resting spot. I am so hot. He is boiling me. Still they went more slowly. She fell through

yellow

enormous canyons of time, down the deep pocket of pleasure, swooning ever more slowly into the depths of delight. She heard dragons roaring, such a slow grinding noise, such a slow turning.

They ate only liquids, some ethereal force seeming to sustain them now, for they lost no weight, but grew light as lamps. His countenance became magical. In his face she saw blue God-masks, jewels, crowns. The sound, the sound of their divine grinding surrounded them. No longer human, they lived outside of time.

The beautiful presence came, as he touched her in the womb, and like spring burst forth. I am creation. From her came the universe, that was the roar. From her came worlds, she was their door. Spread across the galaxies, she moved her body slowly, coming everywhere, at once, very wise.

In the beat of moons, not seconds, he stroked her, so say the Scriptures.

SILK

SLEEPING WITH CATS

■

Marge Piercy

I am at once source
and sink of heat: giver
and taker. I am a vast
soft mountain of slow breathing.
The smells I exude soothe them:
the lingering odor of sex,
of soap, even of perfume,
its afteraroma sunk into skin
mingling with sweat and the traces
of food and drink.

They are curled into flowers
of fur, they are coiled
hot seashells of flesh
in my armpit, around my head

a dark sighing halo.
They are plastered to my side,
a poultice fixing sore muscles
better than a heating pad.
They snuggle up to my sex
purring. They embrace my feet.

Some cats I place like a pillow.
In the morning they rest where
I arranged them, still sleeping.
Some cats start at my head
and end between my legs
like a textbook lover. Some
slip out to prowl the living room
patrolling, restive, then
leap back to fight about
hegemony over my knees.

Every one of them cares
passionately where they sleep
and with whom.

yellow

Sleeping together is a euphemism
for people but tantamount
to marriage for cats.
Mammals together we snuggle
and snore through the cold nights
while the stars swing round
the pole and the great horned
owl hunts for flesh like ours.

GOODNIGHT LADIES

■

Elaine Perry

You draw on my windows
Pictures meant for a museum;
You didn't know the words to introduce yourself.
Now you sit in my house
Quiet as an immigrant putting away her money.
You are a woman living alone like me,
Covering yourself with too many coats.

I read your lips when no light shines on them,
Our bodies overlap, two pages of a letter,
We make a thin veil and cover ourselves
Like lace petticoats under the skirt of a lullaby.

"Finger the runes

For Sexual Instructions"

THE MISSIONARIES EXPLORE CENTRAL ASIA

■

Noel Peattie

Along the yellow Silk Road
our camels knelt in markets, patiently,
for long we sojourned, bargaining
for some good blankets, skins
not leaking, saddles.   These we
did not get, got blankets with holes,
skins with leaks, saddles with creaks,

trading for all these,
Venetian glass (frail), silver (plate),
kettles with hairline cracks.
                              We told the market
we came to preach the Christ.

They offered us girls: in trade
for our camels: shy breasts,
love.   These we refused:
devoted to our camels, and by vows
to poverty, chastity, and not least,
obedience: as priests, to the Lama with three hats,
and, as his subjects, to the Khan
of the two-headed eagle.   All but one

of us. Brother Crispin (twenty-three) confessed
of love, with a girl named Asia—
(or so he called her, so she called herself)
brown niplets, slim legs round his waist
(he cross-legged, straight-backed on her bed)

yellow

her seated sweetness, bird on branch,
her hands—
                    We wouldn't let him go!
on. Broke camp, got him away;
next night, he disappeared.

We struggled East, met helmeted horsemen,
herding us under yellow silk banners.
Father Paulus carried the Cross upright.
I, Timothy, asked for the translation
of yellow banners' big Chinese characters.
Then, one of their eunuch translators:

"HONORED BARBARIAN PRIESTS
CARRYING TRIBUTE TO BUDDHA."

(And Brother Crispin? Him we never
saw again; doubted his tale.
With us no girl's a continent,
no lass's loving half that skilled,
that shameless, —ah,

that sweet.)

SILK

IN THE LAST YEAR OF CHILDHOOD

■

D. Nurkse

We made love
in the basement of the gym
listening to the thud of balls
the whoops and the foul whistle
the metallic voice saying
Time Out: in summer
we had to meet in the cemetery
and lie on a slab
feeling the tiny gap
of the name against
our nakedness—
since the old dictators were dying
we took turns being on top.

HOME FROM THE FAIR

■

D. Nurkse

At twilight in the Greyhound
I spread my Letter jacket over our laps
and she put her hand under my pants
and began humming, while around us
the farmers read or dozed or frowned.
She began chattering about the coming harvest
and I looked out the window
in a cool frenzy as the farms
began to slip away, each
with its pump, bucket and swing
and then there were just fields
and distant fireworks, and it was night
and she began describing the melons
at the 4-H club so eagerly
the farmers unwrapped their enormous sandwiches.

yellow

DO YOU KNOW
THE FACTS
OF LIFE?
(QUIZ)

■

*Lynn Luria-
Sukenick*

Sample question: *Did you ever, as an
adolescent, want to kiss your own mouth
in order to know how you felt to the people you were paired with randomly at
parties, when the opposite sex still seemed
as remote as Egypt? How many of you
still want to kiss your own mouths?*

If you did well on the sample
question, you'll want to take the rest
of this exam. Sample answers are provided to the following
questions in order to keep you company in your ruminations
and to give you encouragement if you hesitate or stray. A final
score will not be tallied in this quiz.

1. *We all know that the origins of sexuality are in the family. Write
a brief essay about sex in your family.*

Her mother, when she's very little, informs her that babies
come from seeds. She inspects every flowerpot in the house to
see if a brother or sister is on its way. Later her mother liberal-
ly expands the information but keeps a strict eye on her growing daughter. In fact, because of her mother's watchfulness
there are many episodes in the girl's childhood of *feelie inter-
ruptus.* Billy Emerson's boy's breath two inches away in a
tantalizing almost. Games of doctor with little red pills and
white caps. And her mother popping up like a doll out of a
Swiss clock, always, at the sexiest moment, calling, "Hi, kids,
milk and cookies!"

2. *What was your first sexual game?*

She is seven years old and she and Barbara Lombardi are
on the porch with their clothes on playing a game they in-
vented called Naked in Hell. They are pretending they have
big firm shapely breasts like movie stars in 1940's sweaters but
they are naked and in hell, where it is all right to be fiendishly
wicked and naked. There is no narrative line in this game
(which is invisible to anyone observing them); the point is to set

SILK

the scene and then feel the tension of the naughtiness, to delight in hours of tumescence and then at dinnertime run into their houses to be little girls in the bosoms of their families. This is the same year that Lana Turner, according to a Hollywood exercise coach, had a perfect body for one week, and four years before Barbara is sexually approached in their neighborhood by a stranger the police fail to apprehend. By then they are eleven years old and she has to walk Barbara home if it's after dark because she's the brave and untouched one. But on the way back, alone, she makes her repel-the-attacker face, grimace of a Japanese actor, while inside of herself she chants, "I'm plain, I'm plain, don't hurt me, don't hurt me," over and over, until she has reached the warm and extended light of her mother's window.

3. *Write an essay on sex and school.*

Richard Krebs, the sixth-grade bully, tells her he can see her when she takes a shower. Although she knows this is impossible, she thinks he may have some apparatus, the kind boys invent and girls don't, that will allow him to see her, so she takes faster and faster showers. Then, apparently overnight, Jerry Smith turns from good boy into dirty joker. "How far is the Old Log Inn? Yuk yuk." She doesn't like the coarseness of the jokes, though she does enjoy the secrecy the jokes are told in. On the way home from school the girls run away from the boys so they can be caught (additional question: *When did* your *cleverness begin?*) and she looks forward to that from lunchtime until three p.m. One day Michael Garrison spreads the rumor that he saw under her skirt when it flew up, but she knows he didn't because he didn't mention the "Tuesday" embroidered in red against white cotton over her appendix. In any case, taunts are compliments in those early days, and the girls thrill to them because they are a sign of interest, an advance over being shunned. This is where confusion begins, and these divisions are reflected, finely honed, even in her recent dreams.

yellow

4. *Relate a recent sexual dream, or several recent sexual dreams.*

She has had two sexual dreams this week, one tantric and one horrific. In the tantric one she's sitting in the archaeologi-calligraphy café with her lover, the sunshine streaming in on ferns and oak tables. There are ancient runes on the walls, the braille of shadows and light. She and her lover finger the runes for sexual instructions which are instantly translated by their bodies into their bodies. In the horrific dream a karate expert chews up pieces of wood until he has crammed his mouth full of splinters. Then he leans forward to kiss her. She wakes up.

5. *Now see what connections exist between sex and sleep.*

She and her lover spend many days in bed   making love   eating leftover Chinese food   playing backgammon   eat-ing pizza   making love   watching Busby Berkeley and *Black Orpheus* on black and white TV he tells her the colors   five days go by and he says "Are you really going all the way into the kitchen? Let me go with you"   reading her Zippy and *King Lear*   playing guitar   it is summer   sultry   a scrim of leaves outside the window   they are singing endless duets of scat in-vented on the spot   they make up a pastime called Scenes You Never Saw writing the erotic passages left out of the great novels   they relinquish themselves to the heat   by accident he knocks her earrings off in his passion   it's all she wears   he al-ways finds them again and places them in her palm   they worry they'll forget how to buy food   go to the bank   read a book   call a friend   you put your forefinger in he says and dial   and *then* what she says   they say hello he says   and then what   their legs are gently pretzeled   they can't get up they giggle they need a servant   they are starving to death   their bodies ache   maggots are in the garbage hairs in the sink the daily papers accumulate at the door of the clapboard house   the air-conditioning's breaking down his spinster cousin whose bed they are in comes back from vacation after they've gone and finds it clean but she has insomnia every night for a whole year.

SILK

6. *Explore the relationship between sex and insomnia.*

She has insomnia, so she's watching the Johnny Carson show. A comedienne is on, horsefaced, skinny, and funny. She was making love with her husband, the comedienne says, when he said, "Say something dirty." She was immediately responsive: "The bathroom," she said, "the kitchen, the living room, the playroom." While she watches TV she thumbs through a paperback someone left behind, *The Coming Celibacy*. Edward, eight months celibate, says, "I'm much more sensitive to things now. For example, I can hear a lot better if there's something wrong with my car." On screen two puppets are enacting an adultery scene, the wife at home is being visited by the milkman. "I can't open the door in my underwear," she says. "You have a door in your underwear?" the milkman replies. "Let me in and I'll help you open it."

7. *Interview one or two of your friends on the subject of underwear.*

"I really like it," says Andrea, putting her feet up on the coffee table. "My all-time favorites were crimson silk with eggshell lace to be seductive for Ted before things got bad between us, then I gave up and wore flannel and wool. Girdles? I did wear a girdle for forty minutes in Shiraz. I had gotten really fat on pistachio nuts and could not get into this blue silk dress and Mother and Dad had to push me into her girdle minutes before the ambassador's party and then I got a stomachache and had to go home and never wore one again."

While talking to Andrea she remembers her honeymoon in Paris, where a friend had warned her about a flourishing white slave trade in lingerie shops: middlemen would snatch you from the cubicle where you were trying on your *soutien-gorge* and sell you into a bordello in the Sahara. She was twenty, her fingers trembling; she fastened the garter belt made of slender strips of lace as her husband stood guard outside, the way he stood guard at the famous hairdresser's, keeping him from cutting

yellow

more than an inch of her waistlength hair, the hair that was so often praised by the artists she posed for back in New York.

8. *Have you ever posed in the nude?*

She works as a model for a few serious New York artists and occasionally for a commercial artist. One night the commercial artist does a series of drawings he hopes to sell to *Playboy* of her reaching, twisting, dreaming into space, all very beautiful, really. It's nighttime, his studio is on the twentieth floor of an office building, luxe and quiet; dead cameras standing around on tripods, two enormous drawing boards, Cartier-Bresson photographs on the walls, humanized hi-tech. Every time she takes a new pose he says, "Great! Great!" It is a strange experience to know that he sees far more in her than what, at that moment, she feels in herself. This, she realizes later, is exactly what it means to be an object. As he keeps busy with pad and charcoal, it frees her to drift and dream. She stares for ten minutes at the face of a Russian woman in one of the photographs until she feels herself lift into an enlightenment she has never felt before. Years later she understands that even meditation has not given her that sense of stillness and of clarity. The artists are not predatory but, on the contrary, protective and fatherly. She feels the air on her naked body as they sketch an image of her onto the soft stretched canvas, and it is as if she is three years old and playing at the shore while her parents sit close by, laughing and eating sandwiches but keeping an eye on her, building her sense of who she is just by being there.

9. *Have you ever posed in the nude with your clothes on?*

He photographs her face while she's telling him a subtly erotic story. It looks like an ordinary picture when it's developed but it excites him every time he looks at it.

SILK

10. *Have you ever attended a pornographic movie?*

She and her husband are parting, a marriage of many years begun in Paris and ending in California, and spend their last evening together at the movies, a common practice among divorcing couples. With a sense of fitness and of humor they attend the program of historical comic erotic movies at the local art cinema, and her annoyance with the banality of those bodies using each other without emotion wins out over her terror and delight in seeing so much active flesh. At the break before the feature an attractive man sits down in the empty seat on her right. Her husband has left in order to go to the men's room. She asks the man if he saw the shorts. "No," he says, he came for the feature. "They were stupefying," she says. It is clear that he enjoys her use of the word "stupefying" and she enjoys his enjoyment of it. They chat a little. Her husband comes back and he and the man exchange mild but indescribable looks. When the lights go out she feels how fully the man fills his seat, and she leans slightly closer to him than to her husband as a symbol of her new life as distinguished from her old. The man moves a fraction closer, and she feels the density of the muscles of his upper arm next to hers. The entire movie is spent adjusting these fractions closer and closer, allowing them to be background to the film and then foreground, eclipsing the film, until at a certain point she and the man simultaneously feel a need to rest, and withdraw, like two sweaty people flung apart to cool after making love. She is surprised at how merry and comforted she feels: he has a solid body; it is very nice. She does not, however, have fantasies that involve sex with strangers. If she'd wanted to be anonymous, she wouldn't have said "stupefying" after all, a word that would set her apart from other people, especially in California.

Reflect on your answers to the questions above and take a ten-minute break.

Begin again with some short answers:

yellow

11. *What is the opposite of an obscene phone call?*

It's a call where you breathe gently, surprise them with kindness, and hang up. A good thing to say is, "Everything you've done up to now has been just fine with me," or "You too will love again."

12. *What is your favorite advice-to-the-lovelorn column?*

She reads in Ann Landers' column a query it will take her at least twenty years to comprehend. "I'm worried," says the correspondent, "because I am pregnant by a man who has slept with so many women I cannot be sure he is the father of my baby."

13. *Now, at your leisure, notice what sexual associations cling to the objects that surround you. Or close your eyes and remember other objects and places you have, at some time in your life, charged with eros.*

Memory is itself sexual, a dionysian attachment to the past accomplished in the face of the scythings of Father Time. She closes her eyes and thinks of: nude beaches; the skin of birches; surfers taking a wave that will never return; damp heaps of russet leaves; *keep cooking till chicken falls off fork;* a willow tree that sinks to its knees as the light subsides; a chemise with green flowers swaying into ivory like the pattern on her grandmother's fine Victorian china, a pattern he liked, the edge of her hand in his mouth, the woods all around, half in darkness, then later the two of them spilled open like loosened yarn or the day she met him in winter sun she said my hands, they're cold, and he took them between his own steepled fingers, the delicious prestige of a first gesture.

Now take a twenty-minute break. During the break, lie down, close your eyes, and imagine your own nakedness. Then, using only your imagination, paint your body until you are covered from the soles of your feet all the way up through your hair. Apply whatever colors seem right to you, by whatever means. When you are finished, lie quietly for a few minutes.

ʃILK

14. *Having relaxed yourself completely, write an essay that is also a confession.*

   A year before the divorce and after long consideration she took a lover—not the usual adultery (guilt, repentance, the stunned mate) but a passion undertaken with her husband's tacit consent. In spite of the consent, whenever her lover called she pulled the phone on its long cord into the walk-in closet and sat among the dresses and skirts and trousers to mute her conversation and to find the privacy she did not want her husband's voice, deep in her head, to encroach upon. Her husband had a suit he liked, a Pierre Cardin that hung in a zippered cover next to where she leaned against the wall to talk on the phone, and she would look abstractedly at the silvery printing on the case, CAR DIN, and think about the rush of traffic outside the hotel where she had last met her lover, and about the novel and graceful allegiances of his golden dreamy body. She would talk to him for hours and emerge from the closet dizzy with the murmur of their voices folded over one another, letting the murmuring seep into her as she lay on the bed in a stupor. One day she reached for her coat in the closet and realized that her dizziness was caused not by her lover's voice but by the mothballs nestled in her husband's suit, their cold insulting sweetness even now seeping into her nostrils and numbing her slightly. Her husband's cleverly accidental control of her while she talked to her lover made her feel she was losing the last of her power, and she decided finally that the marriage was over. The day she packed her bags, a month after she had broken up with her lover because it would be dishonorable to abandon one man simply to go to another, she scooped the mothballs out of the zippered case and replaced them with a dozen candy Easter eggs she had bought that morning at Woolworth's when she was buying her luggage tags. She neatly arranged the yellow and violet eggs under the knifecreased and impeccably silent suit. And then she bit a hole in it.

yellow

15. *Follow this confession with a consideration of the spiritual side of things. What real or imagined encounters have you had with sex gods or goddesses?*

It's November 1st, All-Souls' Day, the day, she thinks to herself, that the dead come back in the form of candy. She's at the local sweet shop, eating chocolate because she's lonely, when suddenly a vision appears. She always hallucinates a little if she eats a lot of chocolate and today she sees a woman in a preshrunk pink punk tee shirt and sheepskin chaps with a banner across her chest that says SEX GODDESS except the S seems to have fallen off. "I'm on a lecture tour," the goddess says. "I talk about how in the Fifties people lay together like flounders and flopped up and down. In the Sixties sex was based on political values; polygamy echoed communal action. In the Eighties everyone carries the burden alone. So promiscuity—from which the word 'prom' was taken—is—"

At the word "prom" a taffeta gown materializes, with a pretty woman in it. "This is Pam," the goddess says, "former prom queen and pom-pom girl."

"Hiya," Pam says, "I hear you're getting divorced. Well honey, you're gonna be lonely. Eat that chocolate. How will you ever live without a man, and I'm telling you, the men out there are all too young, too mean, or married. You'll be singing the blues," she says, and she sashays out humming an old tune in ¼ time, "If you don't like my sweet potato, why did you dig so deep?" The ex-goddess shrugs and, shrugging, vanishes, chaps first.

16. *Write an essay on sex and solitude.*

She decides to prove the prom queen wrong and proceeds to lead a balanced and ascetic life, no chocolate. After several months of this, however, she suddenly loses her tranquility to a lust that her laws against the young, the mean, and the married will not allow her to satisfy. The man dazzles her—red satin flash and life in the f-lane, twenty-four hours a day. Why does she always fall for actors and musicians, the strutting mimes and mummers, the bragging drummers, men dependent on the vulgarisms of amps and artificial lights, when she should be drawn to sonnets and starlight? Violations of good taste have such appeal for her that she wonders whether desire is only a state of disorientation, a matter of breaking sober habits so deeply ingrained that their very disruption seems erotic.

She falls into a state of sexual dyslexia: reading the Bible for courage, she understands it to say that Job is afflicted with sore balls; taking her minerals in the morning, she finds a sodomite on the label where dolomite should be. Hours are lost in fantasy. Finally she imagines going to visit Herbal Cowboy, a healer, making a long trek through the redwoods, home of hippie witches in their covens hovering over their ovens and cauldrons, to his shack in the mountains, where he mixes a concoction and writes a prescription. Her cure, he says, lies in dreaming the same dream night after night, a dream in which she is scrubbing down the steps of the Philadelphia Museum of Art. Eventually the lust will disappear, provided she avoids looking inside the museum—the Kandinskys have a certain bright diaphanous thrust and shatter that might disturb. He also gives her a pass to Wet World, where, having misread "groupers" as "gropers" and then as "groupies" on the giant fishtank plaque, she decides to soothe herself with mammals instead.

She stands at the rim of the porpoise pool and one of the porpoises surfaces and puts his head close to her hand. She strokes his head and his back: it's like petting a giant olive. Intelligence always arouses her sexually, and the porpoise is no exception. She looks into his little eyes and feels herself getting turned on by his brain capacity. The porpoise is attracted by the sheen and shimmer of the satin cowboy shirt she is wearing, and he inches closer, his long nose touching her waist, as if he understands her human silliness and shine. She envisions how lovely it would be to swim with him, speaking in whistles

yellow

and rusty hinge noises, clicks and pingings reverberating through her whole being, touch and sound indistinguishable in the echolalia as they plunge again and again below the mirror of silver waves.

After a day of these fantasies she goes to sleep and she dreams, not about the flashy man who inspired her lust, but about the porpoise. He speaks to her in playful swoops of freshness and rebounds of shyness, his body saying, "Swim with me! Swim with me!" As they swim, the water brilliant and quiet, he nuzzles her, the dark blue depths widening under them. And then, in the voice of a creature who now, involved, fears their differences, who cannot cross a border without vanishing, he says, "Let me go, for the day breaketh," and she lets him go, instantly, and wakes up feeling very clear, her eyes full of tears.

17. *You have almost finished the exam. Conclude it by sitting quietly in a lotus position. Close your eyes and contemplate the ten thousand sensuous things in the physical world. Don't tally your score.*

Notice the white throat of an iris, the quiver of emerald hummingbirds, the rolling gold hills of California summer studded with live oaks. (*What do you consider the most voluptuous season?* Don't rest with the obvious. Maybe it's the late yielding light of autumn, the intimacy in that clarity, the sharpness of light that brings everything closer.) Consider the texture of thin silk velvet, consider the scent of star jasmine, Billie Holiday's voice, any serious tenor saxophonist playing "Body and Soul," Edward Weston's nudes. Georgia O'Keeffe's orchids and lilies. Consider your childhood, the shapes of light in the room, the attentions and rhythms of speech, the fluxes and cuttings, the touch. This is the paradise where generosity begins. Swim with me, swim with me. These are the facts of life. Now, come to your senses.

"I DON'T WANT TO

miss A THING"

There was water east of the house, west of the house,
fields all green.
The one I love lives past those fields.
Rain has fallen on my body, on my hair, as I wait
in the open door for him.

If you aren't already familiar with the above poem, who at first glance would you imagine wrote it? A woman longing for her lover? Guess again. It is a poem written by the great Indian mystic Mirabai to Lord Krishna—that is to say, it is a poem written to the Divine Creative Force, to God if you will.

I think it comes as a surprise to many of us raised in the English-speaking tradition to discover the deeply sensual nature of the religious poetry of other cultures. The idea that the divine can be associated with something akin to sexual passion seems faintly blasphemous. Oh, we find a bit of it in the *Song of Solomon* (neatly reinterpreted as a purely *symbolic* union between Christ and His Church), and a hint in Donne, say, or Blake. But for the most part when we write love poetry, we write it to one another, not to our gods.

Yet in other cultures poetry is full of sexual energy, despite the fact that the poets themselves—Mirabai included—are often strictly celibate. Take, for example, a poem to the Virgin written in Latin by St. Anselm around the year 1078. St. Anselm, by the way, is known as "the father of scholasticism," but you would hardly guess that from the very non-academic passion with which he petitions Mary for grace:

> O highly exalted,
> when the love of my heart tries to follow
>   you,
> where do you go to escape the keenness
>   of my sight?
> O beautiful to gaze upon,
> lovely to contemplate, delightful to love,

yellow

where do you go to evade the grasp of
    my heart?

St. John of the Cross, the great sixteenth-century Spanish ·
mystic, modeled his religious poetry on popular love songs. Lovers
burned with passion while St. John burned with devotion:

O living flame of love!

St. John exclaims,

How lovable, how loving
you waken in my breast,
stirring in nooks, no, none are sharers of.
With your delicious breathing
all health and heavenly rest
how delicately I'm caught afire with love!

As I began to explore the tradition of erotic religious poetry,
I discovered that it was richer and more varied than I'd ever
imagined: Chandidas, Lali, Mirabai, Santa Teresa, St. John,
Goethe—even, with some stretch of the imagination, Anna
Akhmatova, Jules Supervielle, Baudelaire, Andrei Voznesensky,
Shinkichi Takahashi. Everyone I talked to seemed to have an-
other favorite to add to the list.

The question is then: Why do we here in America have so
little erotic poetry with a spiritual consciousness? Where are our
Mirabais and our St. Johns? Are any of those people out on the
street corners with drums and shaved heads writing in their
spare time?

This is not to say that we have nothing at all in the
religious-erotic tradition. Robert Bly (who is one of the best
translators of Mirabai) has given us, among other things, his
"Origin of the Praise of God." We have Dylan Thomas's "Rub
of Love" and Kathryn Van Spanckeren's "Muse Poem." And
I'm sure each of us could name others who have appeared from
time to time, just long enough to give us a taste of what we're
missing. But where are the great cycles, those erotic spiritual

ŞILK

works in which poem after poem radiates St. John's living flame of love?

Are they missing because our society—with some notable exceptions—has simply been too secular to produce cycles of religious poems of *any* nature? Are they missing because, as Susan Griffin and Robert Bly have both suggested, the hatred of women in our culture has for centuries encouraged a distrust of nature and all creative processes? Or are they missing because we all, men and women alike, have trivialized the erotic, chopped it down to size, curtained it off, reduced it to an amusement rather like miniature golf?

On my diningroom wall I have a Tibetan painting that depicts two figures, one male and the other female, enveloped by a cone of fire. It's the fire you see at first, a great conflagration of red and orange that spreads out to the edge of the canvas. Look closer and you see that the man and woman are holding skulls in their hands, and that necklaces of human bones are strung around their necks. The skulls—oddly enough—are smiling. Look closer yet and you realize that the man and woman are making love.

I've been told by an expert on such subjects that this painting represents sudden spiritual Enlightenment, a kind of religious rapture that burns everything in its path. It's a beautiful, terrifying painting, yet I don't look at it often. I think that, like most westerners, I'm afraid to accept the message: that erotic forces are powerful and explosive; that they go far beyond individual human beings; that they are part of that same creative energy that flows through all life; that the world is not neatly divided, as the Greeks would have had us believe, into Eros, Philos, and Agape.

Every morning when I come down to breakfast, that painting reminds me to suspect that for centuries we have all been ignoring a very elemental unity, hiding from it, pretending that we could control something that we've dangerously underestimated. I look at my own poetry, and then I look back at that cone of fire and I hardly know where to begin.

yellow

THE BRIDGE

■

Peter E. Murphy

Unspeakable, the noise under that bridge
as we sat in a circle, opened our flies
and pulled out our small peckers.

There was tons we didn't know, could hardly imagine.
How that curved flabbiness, in love
with its own indifference until things got serious,
could grow majestic and tough
before our eyes.
How someone started dreaming and humming,
chanting a song we all picked up
in our up and down movements.

We sat on a ledge looking over the deep channel,
the ferocious current slapping the concrete columns.
We chanted louder and louder, filling the cavern with music.

SILK

ORCHID FLIGHT

■

*John
Minczeski*

*". . . But even I understood
The Orchid is a bloodless creature
Nothing will ever be so white again . . ."*
　　　　　　—from *Flowers in a Life* by Patricia Hampl

Orchids
A little red vulva, a little red penis.
Lunar moths who know there are 28 ways
to enter the ancient battlefield of night.

Why is the night female? Because orchids are dying.
And because, my love, their strange flight
goes right through me on their way back to Guatemala

and nothing can be done. Leaves blacken
like locust wings that have stopped
sending messages into the world.

And there is so much singing,
so much night, and nobody able to sleep.

yellow

BACKYARD LYRIC

■

*Leslie
Adrienne
Miller*

You can't get here fast enough.
I want to pull you out of the very limbs.
I go out every day and inspect
the little fists. I am ruthless.
Here is where the peonies will be.
I clear and inspect the spot.

Now I wait for the white cheeks
of the lily, the red yawn of the tulip,
and here, oh right in this very tree
I will take armfuls of pink, pinch
them one by one till they come full.

Hurry up, I say. Already the jonquils
are here. I know you know. I want
your footfall, your handfall,
the thin bright lip, ear, thigh.

The cats are doing it.
The frogs are doing it.
And whatever else rustles out there
is doing it. Knock on the door,
call me up, holler at me
from the yard. I don't want to miss
a thing.

"PASSION HAD

reArrANGED
THE room"

AT THE END OF SUMMER

■

*Carolyn
Miller*

All day I have been tired from making love to you,
the muscles in my neck, my inner thighs,
my buttocks, strained and tight. A quiet day,
late September. Home alone, I think of you
off and on throughout the day,
how a dark cloud of hair begins
at your breastbone, your small nipples
hidden in it. How it grows
thickly across your torso, down
your flat stomach to your genitals.

I left you at midnight and walked home.
High above me, a mass of warm moist air from Mexico
was colliding with cold Pacific air.
At three o'clock a huge electrical storm,
like a storm out of my childhood,
ignited in the sky. I stood on my back porch
for a long time, listening to rain and thunder,
watching lightning branch and burn
as if the sky might break open.

The year is moving into autumn; the equinox
is only days away. Weeks ago
people began to say, *well, fall is almost here.*
The mornings have turned darker; both at morning
and at night there is coldness in the air.

I liked looking at you in the light,

yellow

your large hands, the small cave of your navel,
both of us slick with sweat like water mammals,
our hair wet at the roots. You talked to me
as we made love, unhurried. The world is large,
and it is lovely to be kind to one another.

Outside the air is cool, shadowed,
as if the day had a secret. You swim in and out
of my mind from time to time, like making love,
then resting from making love.

SILK

SHE DOES THE RED DRESS DANCE

■

Regina
O'Melveny

She does the red dress dance, sudden topaz turn, pallid
bellies of a thousand frogs dance,   the bishop's
croziered two-step, nightmare's leap, pale nun's severed
black tresses dance,   the centaur's heel and hoof,
telluric crystal pose, Luna moth shudder,   the broken
hands dance, caves of Barcelona step, Dicte candle spiral
down,   the white light wave and particle waltz,
the hand of Fatima feathered unfurl, nausea undulation,
driven Dervish swirl,   the lover's razor cumbia,
Delphic dust hasapiko, Piacenza bronze routine,   the
apples of the black sun dance, Pontian tik, buttock
flap,   the slippery island tarantella, slim fish of
sadness slide,   the hot bride's bounce and cool
gavotte,   the clot in the heavy Aztec heart dance,
swift tongue tango, alchemist's coil, window's cyrtó,
catacombed creep,   the gold-coined shake and Minerva-
bright roll,   the damp place under one hundred breasts
dance, sand draining time and sweet fortune samba,
the red dress, the red dress dance.

yellow

GHOST DANCE

■

*Carole
Maso*

The knock at the door came just as my mother's chestnut coffin was being lowered into the ground again, as my father pivoted in the hard snow, slipping slightly, as my brother brought his hands to his face, and as I—I cannot even see myself anymore. The knock at the door stopped the weeping, stilled the speech in the priest's throat. The knock at the door lifted the horrible weight of snow from my mother's chest and I could breathe again for a moment. I wondered whether I had invented the knock, for it not only stopped her descent now but seemed to tilt her body slightly away from the great silence at the center of the earth. I opened the door slowly, unsure whether anyone would be there at all. I thought this knock might be some elegant safety device of the brain, nothing more. Opening it, though, I still wanted to believe that someone might actually be standing there. Someone who would walk into the room when invited and smile and sit with me for a while. I still wanted to believe that I might not be destined always to hear and see what was not there, love that which did not exist, want what could never be touched.

When I opened the door she was standing there. I had given up the idea of ever seeing her. Over her arm was a dark corduroy coat. She wore a long black-and-white diamonded cardigan, a tailored white shirt and black pants. Her hair was short and dark with a few flecks of gray in it. Her nails were polished and perfectly shaped. She wore a thin, gold band on her right hand. She is real, I thought.

She stared at me, saying nothing. Her mouth was slightly opened but no sound came out. Her eyes were dark. She was still beautiful. I stepped back from her.

"Sabine," I whispered, and tears flowed down my face. "What are you doing here?"

She extended her arm slowly, tentatively, staring at me, never taking her eyes from mine. Her hand was shaking as she touched the side of my face. As she touched me she gasped with that intake, the breath reversing itself. I knew she was real. I could smell her perfume; I could feel her body trembling, her hand was warm.

"I never expected," she said in a thick accent, "I never expected this. I never thought"—her voice trailed off, then came back, "I never thought you'd look so much like her."

"Please," I whispered. "Please don't."

The cat had come to the doorway where we still stood lost in the maze of the complicated past, and rubbed against Sabine's silky leg, then moved in between mine and then back to Sabine. She bent down and picked her up. "China," she sighed, looking at my mother's cat sadly, hugging it to her, burying her face in its fur. "Oh China." In her voice was the sorrow of the universe. In her voice was a car being hit from behind and exploding into fire.

"Please come in," I said.

Sabine, though she said nothing, noticed it all. She recognized the desk, the lamp, the chair, the things my mother had had for years. Some, she had bought with Sabine, over in France.

"I didn't think it would be this hard," she said. "I should not have come."

"No. Sabine. I'm glad you're here. I've always wanted to meet you. I've always wanted to know who you were. To see you. To look at you. To meet you just once. I have all your records," I said shyly and she smiled. I was nervous suddenly. I felt awkward, ill at ease, shaken; I bumped into things. She smiled again. I felt a great disorder moving in. This is not at all how my mother would have acted in such a situation and I thought it brought Sabine some comfort to see me separate from her. But she was still saying it over and over, "I should not have come. I should go."

yellow

"Please don't go," I said.

She nodded her head.

"May I?" she asked, tapping on the top of the scotch bottle.

"Please."

I watched this woman who had never been here before, take charge, finding the glasses, filling them with ice, making the drinks.

"We'll feel better after this, yes?" she said and smiled slightly. She did not sit but did a little pirouette in the center of the room, put her hand to her head and said, "My cigarettes. Ah, yes," and reached into the pocket of her sweater and took out a light blue package. She lit one and her voice deepened with the first drag as she settled into a more familiar place.

"Ah," she said, sinking into my mother's chair. She watched me very closely as we spoke of New York and of Paris, of the house in Maine, her life, her singing—my mother hovering on the periphery of each subject but not mentioned.

"Do you like it here in Greenwich Village?" she asked. She smiled again, absently, weakly. She stood up suddenly and turned her back to me.

"You are so much like her—so beautiful and so sad." Tears fell in her voice. Tears had been falling in her voice a long time it seemed. It was worn by water.

"I should leave."

"Don't go away," I said, touching her back lightly, "please don't go."

With her back still turned away from me, she began snapping her fingers, singing very softly in French, and the room turned dark. Berlin, I thought, "It's Berlin." In the darkness I heard an accordion, a violin, a piano, a drum. "Oubliez," "regardez," "l'histoire," "déjà," "l'amour," "il ne me quitter pas." Each word was rough-edged and it sounded as if it were being pulled from her. She was making the words work as hard as they could, as if she were trying to help herself explain something, as if through these hard, nasal words filled with bitterness something might come clear to her. The accordion faded, the piano, and I listened to that one voice alone in the dark trying to make some sense.

"Jacques Brel," she said, turning to me.

"Another drink?"

I nodded.

"We will feel better soon," she said, wiping a tear from the corner of her eye. She filled our glasses with scotch, took two large gulps, precariously put her glass down, lit a cigarette and sauntered into the bathroom. "We will feel better soon." She began singing again. She reappeared some time later, her eyes heavy with mascara and eyeliner and eyeshadow. Dark lipstick stained her mouth, there was high color in her cheeks. I could not take my eyes off her. She had begun her drunken cabaret dance toward my mother. Swaggering to her in the dark. She was posed in the doorway of death. One hand on her hip, one hand on the frame of the door. "Oh, Christine," she said in her gravelly voice, looking straight ahead, then closing her eyes, rubbing her cheek on her shoulder. "Oh, Christine." She opened them again and looked through the door, closed them, and swerved into her.

"Come here," she whispered and took a few steps forward, moved her shoulder toward me and tossed her head, all style now, all nerve. As she stepped forward her voice took on a different tone; it was a great, consoling hug. "Come here. Oh, please, come."

I moved toward her. "Sabine," I said. We were caught in the dance those who are still alive must do. We were doing what we had to.

"Come here." She was smiling now, laughing almost. "Come here," and under her breath the one word, the unbear-

yellow

able word, the word we could not do without. "Christine." "Come here, Christine." Her look was the look of thirty-five years ago, when my mother was my age and she too was my age. I walked to her, I turned away, I came forward, I hesitated, I moved closer, I stood next to her. She was fearless now. I saw her as my mother must have seen her. She was beautiful and strong.

"Sabine," I said. She looked at me with her twenty-year-old eyes. My mother stood before her again as she ran her hand through my hair and the look did not change back.

I stared at her, grown suddenly young, and as I reached out my hand in a fractured gesture I felt the terrible weight again of my mother's life and I knew what it felt like to be my mother and it hurt more than I could ever have imagined and I let out a small cry.

"Christine, Christine," she whispered. I nodded my head and she touched my dream body. I took her hand in a motion of my mother's, confident, elegant, her lovely hand, her manicured hand, and laid it on my hip where it rested finally. Her soft hand. The trip she had begun thousands of miles away through this long year since my mother's death had ended finally.

I moved her weary hand up my side and onto my breast. She sighed. I wondered what this hand might do with its firm, nostalgic touch.

"Christine," she whispered. "Oh, Christine." I kissed her hand and looked into her dark eyes. She pushed the hair from my face and smiled. Tossed her head away from me like she had done so many times already and looked back, giggling, pouting, squeezing my face in her hands, stroking my head, laughing, pressing me to the floor and lowering her mouth onto mine. She moaned as she kissed me and I moaned back.

"Don't stop," I said as we kissed. "Please don't stop." Her eyes sparkled. Life could be controlled, the world could be managed, true love would not be broken up. Lives would not be wasted, cut short. Things could be held in place. I loved her very much in that moment with her great saving kisses as she pressed her body, that suggested everything, onto mine. I loved her as my mother must have. Here, now, everything fell into simple order. Her soft mouth against mine. Her breasts. Her legs wrapped around my hips. A voluptuous sorrow was propelling us now into a darkness so great, so complete that I could feel it entering me even as Sabine slowly unzipped my dress and I unbuttoned her blouse and put my mouth to her brown nipple. With each movement now we were going deeper and deeper into that darkness, where we might be with her again.

"I will see you again," I whispered, moving my hand to that wonderful, moist place between Sabine's legs. I was losing sight. She touched me gently, kissing me everywhere. Licking me. And the silence deepened and the darkness moved closer. My mother was calling us from far off. Her voice came nearer as we kissed long and deep. Her voice moved into my mouth. "Sabine," I said. For a moment she was with us, in me or I in her, in the center of that darkness where she was still alive and we talked to her.

"I love you," Sabine said. "I've missed you so much. I love you, Christine."

She was warm and safe and she put her great arms around us in the dark. "I love you," I said. She kissed my ear.

But then the light started coming back, quite suddenly, in a matter of seconds. "Mommy," I said and I began to cry. Sabine's eyes were closed but she too was crying when she heard my voice and knew. She did not open them for a long time but when she finally did she saw I was not Christine and she began to sob. She touched my face, hating what her own hands told her.

Our bodies were so heavy with sadness it seemed they might fall through the three floors of the building and onto the

yellow

street. Though we lay perfectly still, I felt my body of lead to be falling.

She lifted herself up finally, very slowly, propped herself up on the window sill and lit a cigarette. It was so heavy she could hardly hold it, barely lift the match, barely exhale and when she did the smoke did not rise. She managed with great effort to get one leg up on the sill, the other dangled in the mournful air. I crawled to her, opened her legs and began gently to kiss her again. She stretched out on the sill like a cat, arched her back, put her hands behind my head and pressed me deep inside her. I could feel her purring under my tongue.

"Ah, ah," was her love call in French to the other side of death where my mother was, whole, smiling, waiting for us. "Ah," she said, lifting my face up and seeing my mother again in her calm, even gaze. She smiled. Dipping into me, her sighs were muffled by my flesh as she slid down the sill, took my breasts in her mouth, kissed my stomach, pushed open my legs, taking me along to the place where it was safe. We moved very slowly, carefully, deliberately and the descent this time offered great pleasure as we burned slowly into a fine ash. To be a fine ash with her. To die. To be nothing but ash. To mix together. To end.

There was rest in that gray, ashen place. We were up to our waists deep in ashes until our waists dissolved too and we were not anything anymore. Nothing. No one. Ash on top of ash on top of ash with her.

From that ash, the world rose up again and called us back, shaped us and we could not ignore its round call and we were back in my room and we knew that she was far, far away. Betrayed, I gave out a long, loud wordless cry into the empty space and the tears began. "Sabine," I cried. Her name came back again. I hated it.

"Oh, Sabine," I said. She shook her head sadly, put a finger, for the world insisted on fingers and we could do nothing about it, she put a finger to my sticky, swollen mouth and outlined it.

SILK

"I will run us a bath," she said. "Nice warm water." I followed her porcelain voice into the bathroom, where she turned on the tub and took from her purse cologne, which she poured into the running water. It was a scent I knew well. My mother always smelled of it when she returned from France, her hair, her clothes, everything in her suitcase. Sabine sat on the floor next to the tub and moved her hand back and forth through the running water, saying nothing, shaking her head and moving her hand back and forth in a solitary motion. She turned to me and in her low, blurry voice, not the porcelain voice anymore, she said, "I need you, Vanessa. I need you, now."

"I need you too," I said and on the cold tile floor, the water still running in the tub, we worked hard with great urgency to it, to that place. "I want to hear you scream," I said.

"Please make me scream," she said.

"Yes," I said. I felt a great rage rising in me. It grew and grew. There was no stopping it. It had no boundaries. No bottom or top. No sides. It would live forever, I thought.

And around us the accident whirled and around us the poems, the best poems, and we felt the rage grow even greater and the waste. And Sabine's giant singing voice. And arms and legs flayed and flew apart.

And the water overflowed. And she screamed.

"I can go on," she said breathlessly. Like sorrow, a woman's body was inexhaustible, like certain kinds of love. "I can go on and on." She touched me with her strong, trembling hand and we made our way again toward the place where she would be and then past her into emptiness where we could live for a few precious seconds alone, without her. Having never known her. Never heard her voice or seen her face. We were tireless. Strong. We would do it. We would fuck our way through her and past her. We would reach it—we had worked so long and hard to get there. I felt the movement from sorrow to anger there in the dark as I bit her shoulder and thrashed against her.

YELLOW

■

"Think," I said, as she thrust herself deep inside of me and I felt myself breaking apart with her body hard against mine, "think," I said as she went deeper and deeper. "Think you can explode into a million pieces and disappear?" I said to my mother, who stood before me. "Who do you think you are?"

I will lose you. I will stop loving you so much. I will forget everything. I will forget. And then there was nothing. No floor. No Sabine. No. I will lose you. Lose. Lose you.

There was nothing. We held on tightly. Two bodies. No names. No places. Nothing to feel sorry about. Nothing to mourn. Nothing at all.

The darkness was kind. The darkness invited me in and I sunk gladly into it and did not rise up and did not move.

I don't know how long it was but after a while I began to smell her again. Her warm, soaking body. I smelled her cologne like spices, I smelled her hair and then I felt her touching me. Light filtered through the blinds. I could see every branch on every tree. I saw the cracks on the plaster ceiling. I was coming back to the world—where she did not exist anymore. The world where she—

"No," I whispered. I heard the radio. "Already it is snowing in seven states," a man's voice said. I was back in the life where she was dead. Where she felt no cold. No snow. Not there. She was not there. I looked at Sabine. She too was back. I looked into her large, inconsolable eyes. "Why, Sabine?" I asked, holding her tightly. "Why?"

We fucked with the ferocity of my mother's death over and over again. We moved from the floor to the tub. From the tub to the bed. "Exhaust me," I begged. "Let me rest." We dragged our grieving bodies over every inch of my apartment, lost ourselves, saw ourselves differently, changed the ending to the story for a while, but we always returned. We became gentler, then rougher, then gentler again. Only our lovemaking could relieve the pain and longing that each of us had created in the other. The warm liquid our bodies gave up changed the atmosphere. It was smelly and dreamy and we floated in the world our sorrow made. We explored long into the day every curve, every contour of it.

"Speak only in French," I told her.
"Say nothing but with your eyes," she said.
"Don't move or I'll stop."
"Sing me a song."
"Now you sing me one."
"Turn over on your back."
"Put your hair up in a bun."
"Put on your mother's pearls and high heels."
"Let me kiss your ankles."
"Let me drench you in cologne."
"Let me kiss you everywhere."
"Make it all stop."
"Make everything disappear, please."

Day turned into night and night gave way to dawn and dawn to day until we were finally able to sleep in light, entwined. When I finally woke up it was dark out. She was sitting up in bed smoking. She turned her head toward me.

"How could I help but love you?" she whispered, smoothing down my wild hair with her hand. I smiled. She reached over me and turned on the light. Passion had rearranged the room. We had broken things. Books were strewn across the floor. There were empty bottles everywhere. Broken cologne bottles, wine bottles, scotch bottles. Dark marks striped the walls as if fingers had been dragged down them searching for the way out. Sharp black shards, her records were stuck in the bed. My mother's poems too, everywhere, torn from her books. I closed my eyes.

"How could I help but love you?" she said. The sheets were still damp. I put my face in the pillow. I felt some peace.

yellow

"I fed China," she whispered. "We are old friends. Are you hungry?" she asked.

"No, not really."

"What time is it?"

She shrugged. "I have to leave in the morning."

"Have you been up long?"

"No," she said.

We spoke very quietly and barely moved so as not to disturb the calm. We thought that if we did not draw attention to ourselves, if we did not alert sorrow, it might not seek us out.

"Why didn't you come to the funeral?" I asked very, very quietly.

"The press," she said. "I couldn't bear to face them."

I nodded.

"It was very hard. Fletcher punched one reporter. I never saw Fletcher punch anyone before." We lay in silence for a long time. Even though we were quiet and did not move, it was coming to get us. I thought of the press. How they described us all. All the things Fletcher said.

"No, that's not really it," she said finally. "The real reason I did not come was Michael. Your father loved her as much as I did. It would not have been fair to him. It would have hurt too much." She looked away. "Fletcher is in New York too, yes?"

"No, Sabine. He's still in the Black Hills. On the reservation. I never hear from him anymore. Sometimes I think I've lost him for good. All my letters have been returned."

Sometimes I imagine my brother's massive, muscled arm pointing those letters back to me, refusing this world.

"C'est étrange. Je ne sais—"

"I miss him, Sabine."

"Oui," she said, "bien sûr."

She was slipping into French. She looked tired but calm. She sat straight up in the bed now, leaned over me and looked into my eyes. She had come to tell me this, whatever it was she was about to say.

"Vanessa," she said. "Do you know, Vanessa . . ."

I could see it in her posture. I could hear it in the changed cadence of her speech. In the pauses around her words. The way her voice wavered, faltered suddenly. There was quiet and out of the quiet she finally said, "Your mother loved you so much." The words hung in the night like stars where I could see them shining. "She loved you so much. I wonder if you have any idea at all. She wanted you more than anything in the world." She paused. "Did she ever tell you about that afternoon at the psychiatrist's?"

I shook my head. Sabine could not know. My mother had died. She had told me nothing. She was always so mysterious, a retreating, exhausted figure, deceptively close but when I tried to talk to her or reach out my hand I could never touch her.

"Christine had just learned she was pregnant with you a few days before. We were in New York together for the weekend and she had an appointment at the psychiatrist's. She never talked about what went on there, but she seemed very nervous about going this time and she asked if I would come with her. So of course I did." Sabine lit a cigarette. "It was an office on Madison Avenue."

"I know where it is," I said.

"A beautiful view, modern, very chic, the way only New York can really be."

I thought of my mother walking into that office with its thick carpets and glass tables and how the objects in the room must have seemed to float before her eyes and how frightened she must have been.

"The psychiatrist came out and told Christine to come in. He was very tall and he bowed his balding head as he spoke. He spoke in a very quiet, reassuring voice. I had never seen

yellow

your mother so panicked. It was not like her to show it, but she could not control herself this day. 'I will not come in without Sabine,' she said. 'Very well then,' he smiled in his kind, patient way and we both went in. His office was very large and elegant. Very beige. Magnificent."

I saw my mother, as Sabine spoke, sinking into the beige carpet as if it were quicksand. I, too, minute inside my mother, must have sunk with her as he closed the door.

" 'I've just received the results from your pregnancy test,' he said gently. 'I think that it is important for us to talk about it right away.' Your mother was shaking.

"And then he said, 'I have told you many times that a child is not a good idea for you at this time. I am being prudent and conservative in my judgement, I believe. You are in precarious mental health and cannot go off your medication now. I must recommend that you do not have this baby. I can arrange everything for you. It will be quite painless and it will be safe. I am only telling you what I truly believe is best.'

"Your mother stood up. She was not shaking anymore.

" 'Prudent,' she said, evenly. 'Conservative. Not have this baby.' " And I knew how her mouth shaped to hold that word, baby.

" 'I will have children. I will write poetry. There is nothing you can do about it.' "

My mother grows large and rises above the carpet. The floating objects of the room spin into her hands and she smashes them against the great, wide, Upper East Side windows, and speaks now from the clarity at the center of her anger. "I will have children. I will write poetry. There is nothing you can do about it."

"She was radiant," Sabine said. "She rubbed her belly through her dress and moved about the room furiously like an animal protecting her unborn, snarling at the man. In her dazzling anger. In her crystalline, in her jewel-like anger. 'I will have children,' she stated, lucid in the perfection of her anger.

SILK

"And she threw the objects of art at the psychiatrist," Sabine said, "and hissed at him until he was silent.

"She could be very cruel, you know," she said.

"Yes, I know."

"But she could never really be cruel to us." Sabine smiled slightly. "She was still raging out on the street, so much so that I was afraid she might lose you, right then, and I said to her, I remember it perfectly, I said to her, 'If you don't calm down, my love, that beautiful baby of yours is going to be born angry and fighting.' She looked at me. Her eyes were purple and wild and she said to me in perfect control, 'If she's lucky. Oh, Sabine, she'd be very lucky to be born fighting.'

"And here you are now. All grown up." She brushed me as she got back under the covers and lay close to me. Her leg rubbed against mine. The night pressed down hard on us and for a long while we just lay there looking at each other and saying nothing. The radio played late-night music. We could hear the muffled honks of horns. Sabine kissed me on the shoulders. On the neck. On the mouth and I felt the slow, circular motion away once more. We were very gentle with each other, careful. We were fragile, precious items, easily broken. We were very tender this time. There was so much pleasure now and it grew slowly more and more intense. We gave up again, just once more before we became brave. The feeling of finality now in this act made us want to prolong it and we did for hours and hours of slow, careful pleasure. Explored one last time every curve, every bone, every trembling. Then quiet. Stillness. Peace. Finally.

The sun was rising. It was getting light outside. In slow motion Sabine got out of the bed and began dressing.

She got back under the covers fully dressed and lay next to me. She kissed my forehead, my cheeks, my neck, my bare shoulders. "Ah, Vanessa," she said in her quietest voice, running her finger up my arm, my needle-marked arm, the punc-

yellow

tured vein: "this would break your mother's heart. Your mother was not afraid to suffer. She never gave up, even in the face of terrible sadness. She was always brave. And she asked that we be brave with her." Sabine turned toward the wall.

"I know," I whispered and hugged her shoulders and kissed her ear. "I know, Sabine."

We lay very still in silence. The sky was white. It had started to snow. I could feel the white struggling to enter the holes in my arms. I crossed them. Sabine stared out the window. With each flake on the pane she seemed to be moving farther and farther north. When she began to speak again her voice was not audible. The snow had taken it away from her. Only gradually did it become something I could hear.

"It had snowed overnight," she sighed. "Your mother slept late that morning for her, until about ten o'clock. When she woke I pulled up the shade. She was so thrilled with the whiteness of the landscape. It had been a complete surprise. I remember that morning as perfectly as if it were yesterday: the beautiful light in that house in Maine and Christine in her robe looking out the window out into the whiteness, the vastness. She was fascinated, spellbound almost, very preoccupied. She had one of her faraway looks on her face. You know how she could look sometimes." I though of my mother burying herself in that snow as she looked out the window.

"But then she pulled away from whatever it was she saw and in a voice I will never forget she said, 'This is what I've wanted all along. This peace, finally. All this,' and she motioned into the air. 'You, Michael, the children. And this calm. This is what I've wanted,' and she looked back into the snow and put her hand in mine. That was the last morning I would ever see her. Next week she'll be dead one year. The last thing I remember her saying to me," and she smiled slightly and said every word slowly like a prayer, " 'This is what I wanted.' "

Sabine closed her eyes. "We were lovers for thirty-five

years." I looked at Sabine, her head that had not left my mother's shoulder, the arm that cradled the neck still.

"Did Daddy know?" I whispered.

"Oh yes. He knew all along. The only thing he ever wanted was that she be happy."

"But wasn't it hard to always love her from such a distance, Sabine?"

She gazes off. Her thoughts are in French. She puts on her coat. I am not really waiting for an answer. I see us differently now, not like before but from what I assume the real angle is, the angle my mother must see us from. I picture us from far above. Sabine and I are very small. I open the door and she kisses me in the hallway and says something that is inaudible from such a distance and turns to leave, looking back at me several times and waving as she saunters down the hall. From that angle we are laughable, pathetic, pitiable. From that angle we don't have a chance. From that angle it is clear we are doomed.

"But wasn't it hard to love her from such a distance?" The question lingers.

"No," Sabine says, walking back to me, and the vision breaks. "It was not really so hard."

There are other angles. There are other ways of seeing.

"No," she says again. She takes my hand and holds it tightly. Squeezes my hand. "Vanessa," she says, and I see her straight on now. She is an enormous, brave figure, this small woman who holds my hand. She is a figure of extraordinary courage.

"Vanessa," she says and her voice is strong, fierce. "We must learn to love her from here now." She hugs me tightly. "Oh, Vanessa," she says and a great tenderness floods her voice, her whole body, which I hold in my arms in this last embrace. "We must learn to love her from here."

"AND NOW THE TWO

OF YOU ARE FISH"

BESTIALITY

■

Rebecca Meketa

We've both lost
7 lbs.
because
we've done nothing now
for three weeks
but fuck.
Me
clinging possum-style
to your bellyside
coming like a yawn.
& how I lust
for a long hairless tail
to wrap 'round & 'round
your thick   hard   thigh.

yellow

INDIGO'S MARVELOUS MOMENT

■

Ntozake Shange

(Indigo, a young girl whose best friends, companions and confidants are her hand-sewn dolls, has ventured out for a visit to the Colored Methodist Episcopal Church and its garden-keeper Sister Mary Louise.)

"I told you awready. You too big to be talking to dolls. Good Lord, Indigo, look at yourself." Indigo tried to focus on Sister Mary's face. But she only saw a glimmering. She tried to look at herself, and kept blinking her eyes, rubbing her palms over them, to get some focus. She saw something spreading out of her in a large scarlet pool at her feet. Sister Mary jumped up and down.

"Indigo, the Lord's called you to be a woman. Look on High for His Blessing. Look, I say. Look to Jesus, who has 'blessed you this day.'" Indigo fell down on her knees like Sister Mary had. And listened and swayed in her growing scarlet lake to the voice of this green-eyed woman singing for the heavens: "Trouble in Mind," "Done Made My Vow," and "Rise and Shine," so that Indigo would know "among whom was Mary Magdalene."

"Speak, child, raise your voice that the Lord May Know You as the Woman You Are."

Then Sister Mary Louise rose, her thin body coated with Indigo's blood. She gently took off Indigo's clothes, dropped them in a pail of cold water. She bathed Indigo in a hot tub filled with rose petals: white, red, and yellow floating around a new woman. She made Indigo a garland of flowers, and motioned for her to go into the back yard.

"There in the garden, among God's other beauties, you should spend these first hours. Eve's curse threw us out of the garden. But like I told you, women tend to beauty and children. Now you can do both. Take your blessing and let your blood flow among the roses. Squat like you will when you give birth. Smile like you will when God chooses to give you a woman's pleasure. Go now, like I say. Be not afraid of your nakedness."

Then Sister Mary shut the back door. Indigo sat bleeding among the roses, fragrant and filled with grace.

Marvelous Menstruating Moments

(As Told by Indigo to Her Dolls as She Made Each and Every One of Them a Personal Menstruation Pad of Velvet)

Flowing:
When you first realize your blood has come, smile; an honest smile, for you are about to have an intense union with your magic. This is a private time, a special time, for thinking and dreaming. Change your bedsheet to the ones that are your favorite. Sleep with a laurel leaf under your head. Take baths in wild hyssop, white water lilies. Listen for the voices of your visions; they are nearby. Let annoying people, draining worries, fall away as your body lets what she doesn't need go from her. Remember that you are a river; your banks are red honey where the Moon wanders.

yellow

SKIN DIVER

■

Mary Mackey

swimming in the Caribbean
I saw a manta ray
rise from the sand
and ripple the great
wing of her body
through the glass-blue
water

and my breath
caught against the bubble of
my throat
as she moved out
beyond the reef
into the inconceivable black push
of the open sea

I have gone down for her since
my manta
again and again
fished the dark waters
of my night dreams
and the shallow reefs
of my days

I have tracked her
through salt, and sleep
and love
felt her tremble
in the flesh
of a strong man
gone gentle
felt her lift
and fall back again
like the thrust
of the waves

SILK

I have imagined
that if I opened my eyes
quickly she would
be there above me
dark circle of flesh
carved out of my sky
primordial as the
first contraction of passion
complete in herself
as a piece of whole cloth

she is my dark lady
this fish
I feel her absence
as parted lovers feel
the phantom pressure
of each other's bodies
I miss her
as I miss the dead
I have loved
I look for her
in the eyes of strangers
I curse the water
that leaves no tracks

I wait for her return
as I wait
for my own youth
to come back to me
swimming in one morning
salt-crusted
on the first heave of the tide.

yellow

DON'T START SOMETHING YOU CAN'T FINISH

■

Mary Mackey

Time travel is easy
take a good look at anything
but be careful
the holes in a button
can become the mouths
of dead relatives
discussing Harry Truman
sweating and smelling of soap
they lean close to one another
their breath sweet and heavy
flies hover above them
like halos
om-buzzing the metal spoon
by your baby hand
into a moon or a silver dollar
or the tin dipper
your lover drank out of
fifty years before
when you were both chopping cotton
for Mr. Delapreux
up to your ankles in red mud
sixteen and both of you
wet as a field
and him grabbing you by the waist
and sinking and sinking
into that soft grass you went
with each other's salt on your tongues
and suddenly you're lions
turning each other over
in the dust
maybe this is a hundred years ago
maybe a thousand
you can't tell
you can smell zebras
—a very sexy smell—

and you lash your long tail
and he opens his great red mouth
to give you a love nip
only the red of his throat
gets loose and swells
and fills up everything
and look out
he's a poppy
and so are you
and your passion
is reduced to tossing pollen
at each other's stamens
under a sky so clear
it reminds you of water
which it is, of course,
and now the two of you are fish
not a penis or a breast in sight
and you're nosing in coral sand
on some godforsaken reef
erecting your fins
and dancing around each other
planting your eggs
and milky white seeds
in little bubbles of mucus
that stick together like balloons
and when you try to stop
the transformations
things only get worse
and now you're some asexual
budding thing
and now you're an *E. coli*
in William Hurt's small intestine
and you're saying about
sixteen acts of contrition
and swearing off sex altogether

yellow

but it's too late
because your DNA is all unraveling
and replicating
and it feels great
like tongues touching
like that button you were looking at
in the first place
that fatal button
on your jeans
that fatal row of buttons
being undone
ever so slowly
one by one.

CHINA

■

Dorianne Laux

From behind he looks like a man
I once loved, that hangdog slouch
to his jeans, a sweater vest, his neck
thick-veined as a horse cock, a halo
of chopped curls.

He orders coffee and searches
his pockets, first in front, then
from behind, a long finger sliding
into the slitted denim like that man
slipped his thumb into me one summer
as we lay after love, our freckled
bodies two plump starfish on the sheets.

Semen leaked and pooled in his palm
as he moved his thumb slowly, not
to excite me, just to affirm
he'd been there.

I have loved other men since, taken
them into my mouth like a warm vowel,
lain beneath them and watched their irises
float like small worlds in their open eyes.

But this man pressed his thumb
toward the tail of my spine
like he was entering
China, or a ripe papaya,
so that now when I think of love
I think of this.

"& DON'T I

LOVE TO
NUZZLE"

SRNGARARASA: IN THE EROTIC MOOD

■

Steve Kowit

1

Where the swollen Monongahela
washes the Alleghenies
wind perfumes the air with fine pollen
& butterflies flicker among the vines
& birds
abandoning all modesty
sing of paradise
in the cool branches.
Here young girls
whirl about on the hillside,
their summer dresses
billowing out
like colorful petals.
Shortly, young men will join them
& they will shriek with delight
& chase each other
& dance
& couple
by couple vanish
into the swaying field
where honey-bees feast
on the bells
of delicate flowers

after Jayadeva

yellow

2

Mother, it's the freezing wind
that's brought such color to my cheeks
& disarrayed my hair
& made my lips so tender.
Why this woolen scarf
has even bruised my throat
see—look here—
No, mama, I swear it—
I have spent the afternoon alone!

after Dharmadasa

3

Let the fire of my passion
glow in the eyes of my beloved.
Let it illuminate her path.
Let the liquid
of which my body is composed
be the river refreshing her
& the well
at which she quenches her thirst.
Let my spirit be the air
she breathes
& thru which she moves
till we are no longer ourselves
& I lie by her side in the earth.
Let our dusts be one.

after Govindadasa

AUGUSTINE'S LAST DAYS

■

Lance Olsen

Smoke stains the lemon sky to the east of Hippo where the barbarians have pitched hundreds of small camps.

No one saw them come. Dark curls appeared from nowhere about a week ago.

The city magistrates have sent a party with news of the affair to Rome, asking for auxiliaries, but even if the messengers journey safely it will take months for the troops to arrive. And so the citizens do nothing but wait, pass time reinforcing the clay walls, barricading the main gate, doubling the guard.

And Augustine sits at his writing desk in the tower, his dry cheek cradled in palm, staring at smoke-smears, staring at the perfectly blue sea to the northeast, trying and failing again and again to forge ahead with his new work.

Una, his concubine, sprawls spread-eagle on the bed, plucking at her lyre.

When Augustine is anxious he makes love more often. Now Una is exhausted. Recently it has been daily, after meals, between meals, during meals. Faint blue bruises radiate from finger- and teethprints on her neck, shoulders, buttocks. Pale pink scratch shadows crisscross Augustine's otherwise white back and flabby thighs.

Augustine makes love as though his life depended on it.

He buries his face in her jasmine-scented hair, squeezes his eyes shut, grimaces as though lifting a horse, and daydreams of a small dark figure surrounded by some sort of birds (hummingbirds? nightingales? sparrows?), daydreams of thousands and thousands of pear trees in an unknowable number of exquisitely straight rows.

Augustine: almost eighty; almost bald, save for a white wisp of hair behind each large and bristly ear; swollen knuckles; bad feet; teeth rattling around in a sore jaw; hazy vision on the

yellow

best of days; a lover of pears; a lover of lovemaking; a taker of finely ground monkey glands (sprinkled on meats, dissolved in red wines and water, massaged on his member) in a furious attempt to increase sexual strength, to augment endurance, to defuse the diurnal pulse of anxiety.

In the middle of the night Augustine gets up, feet aching, teeth throbbing, and shuffles over to the desk by the window. Stars twist in the sky. A weak orange glow in the east. He searches for a scrap of paper, writes out in shakey script one line. *Oh God, grant my celibacy, but not yet.* Then he shuffles back to bed.

Una: almost forty; almost firm; a fancy of fine long brown hair; glittering brown eyes; a slight mole raised on her left shoulder; another (slighter still) raised over her left eye; breasts that have thought about sagging for a long long time; a lover of the lyre; a lover of the theologian; a student of the theologian, who met her when she was almost twenty and he almost sixty and a teacher of rhetoric in Milan. She was a private student, he her tutor. They walked a labyrinth of narrow streets, the brilliant sun stinging the backs of their necks, discussing Joseph and Job, the lovely dream of Scipio, Aeneas and Dido, the parables, Trimalchio, Constantine, Julian the Apostate, all those years of political spasms and military collapses. They sat in restaurants, among forests of thick plants, and ate extravagantly. Una brought Augustine flowers. Augustine brought Una to Carthage, Madaura, Sitifis, Caesaria, playing on the beaches under a white sun and in the turquoise ripples. She was a terrible student. He was a terrible teacher. She forgot assignments, could not write to save her life, could not talk about ideas, broke down in tears at the slightest provocation. He stormed, cursed, threatened, shouted, stamped. One evening on their way home from an elegant restaurant they stopped in an alley and Una turned to Augustine and kissed him. He hugged her

tightly. She uttered an abrupt fart. —Indigestion, she said.
—Love, said Augustine.

Three weeks after the first dark curls from the camps, store keepers step out of their houses in the morning mist to find the wheels of their carts broken. Clothes begin vanishing off lines strung between apartments two floors from the ground. Ugly words and obscene sketches are scrawled across walls. Small steaming piles of human feces show up in the middle of streets. Somehow the barbarians have found a way to slip into the town at night, to wander among the unprotected citizens. But no tunnels are found, no ladders by the walls, no ropes, no flaws. More guards are posted. One night a small fire breaks out in back of the library, and several shelves of books are damaged before it is extinguished. There is talk about sending another party to Rome, talk that the first party may have been intercepted, but everyone knows it is too late for that.

The tallest tower in Hippo, made of caked clay and heavy timber, with a view of the eastern horizon and a square of sea and sky and city: a twelve-by-twelve attic room filled with the overly sweet scent of jasmine and the sour smell of monkey gland: a large bed of straw and an oak desk (covered with manuscripts, pens, dried flowers, assorted jars, three half-burned candles, a primate's skull) and three walls of book cases packed with papers: dirty white walls, dirty white ceiling, timber floor with a trapdoor in the middle of it: one body, older, very much older, sitting in a chair at the desk, rubbing swollen knuckles, and another body across the room, sprawled in straw, spinning a trill of notes.

Una breaks off playing and giggles.
—What? Augustine says.
He rummages through his bookshelves, pulling out manuscript after manuscript, searching for a quote he barely remembers.

yellow

—Nothing.

—No, what?

—I just thought of another joke.

—Tell me.

—You won't like it.

—I'll like it. Tell it to me.

—Okay. Here goes. What do you do with a dog that doesn't have any legs?

—I don't know. What?

—Take it for a drag.

Augustine pauses, look up.

—Foul, Una. Extremely foul.

—Actually I had thought it rather canine.

Her heavy breasts jiggle as she laughs.

Sometimes when Augustine writes, Una lies in bed and stretches herself so that she may feel less alone.

If a man does not love the happy life, he certainly does not possess it. And besides, if he does love it and possess it, he must needs love it more than all other things, since everything else that he loves must be loved for the sake of the happy life. Again, if it is loved as much as it deserves to be loved (and a man cannot be happy unless he loves that life as it deserves), the man who so loves it must inevitably wish it to be eternal. Therefore life will only be truly happy when it is eternal.

One evening a seven-year-old girl, who had been playing with some friends near the city gate, does not come home for dinner. An alarm is sounded, all the citizens turn out for the search, but nothing is found of her. She has vanished. At dawn she turns up, curled in a ball, on the doorstep of the magistrate. She has been raped and her nose broken. Smudges of blood appear on her thighs. A thin trickle slips down by her mouth. When questioned, she can't remember what happened. Two opinions form: the majority are convinced that the Vandals stole her and raped her; but some maintain one of the townies is to blame. In any case, a curfew is set for sundown. Next day a second party is sent out of the city gates, towards Rome.

Augusine sits bolt upright in the darkness, his heart pulsing quickly, his teeth screaming, a brilliant premonition dazzling the inside of his head: the image of a small dark figure drifting in a flock of unrecognizable birds; the image of an unbelievably square orchard of pear trees, twenty trees by twenty trees, four feet between each tree, clearly visible grains of dust on each yellowish green piece of fruit beneath a white sun.

Augustine and his concubine lie in straw one afternoon, munching on oranges, bananas, cantaloupes (sweet fluid dripping from their mouths), drinking white wine, the old theologian guffawing, his old white buttocks shaking, the aging woman cupping her breasts because they have bobbed so much they hurt, a warm breeze from the sea wafting over them.
They are having a flatulation competition.
—*Poof!* goes Una.
—*Fffffffffffffff!* goes Augustine.
—*Pft!*
—*Brrrrrrrrrrrrupupupupup!*
—*Thwip. Pip. Pip.*
Augustine reaches over for the box of matches and strikes one.
—*Beeeeeeeeeeeeee!*
But then:
—*Yeeeeeeeha! Cheeeeeeeeeeeee-rist!*
A thin blue flame shoots out across the bedspread.
Una doubles over with joy.
Augustine is up and out of bed, dancing around the room, fanning his bottom and squawking like a shot goose.
—I've burnt my bum! I've burnt my bum!
—Fried lice.

yellow

—You laugh! I've frazzled my fanny! I've torched my
tuchis! I've flamed my *Furzmacher!*

—Ah, my dear, you are simply combustible.

—Inflammable.

—You burn me up.

—You burn *me* up.

—Are you in pain?

—My hairs are frizzled. They shall never stand again. I've
got bumus blisters.

—Rump roast?

—A fry by night.

—Ah, sweetheart.

—Sweetfart.

—This is divine, my love, this is heaven.

Augustine hobbles back to bed, crawls in beside Una, buries his head in her hair.

—Almost, he murmurs, almost.

—Hairy Mac, she says, you are a king.

—Sucky Moll, Sucky Moll, and you are a queen.

Over the next few weeks the food begins running low.
Stores are broken into. Wells begin drying up, the water thick
and salty.

Lots are drawn. A well-armed group of men is sent outside
the city walls to hunt and collect roots. They do not return.
Some say the barbarians found them, others that they fled.

Several high officials talk of packing up what they have
left, arming themselves as well as possible, and setting forth in
a caravan. Within a week they could reach Madaura. But the
horrible idea arises that this attack may not be an isolated one,
that other cities are under siege too. Better, it is agreed, to wait
for reinforcements. They will be coming any day.

Children's stomachs begin bloating from malnutrition. Their
eyes turn dull and yellow. Their skin turns the consistency of

leather. Purple sores erupt on their gums. White scales, like those from a fish, appear in their hair.

Another young girl is raped. This time a chunk of flesh has been gnawed off the girl's shoulder and she has fallen into shock. The next day a number of citizens have vanished. Rumors circulate that they have climbed over the walls during the night in an attempt to flee. They never reappear.

Perhaps birds, perhaps swallows or herons or hummingbirds. With such bad eyes it is hard to tell. Perhaps not birds at all. Perhaps butterflies. Perhaps a glorious swarm of butterflies.

At twilight a single man stands before the gates of the city. He is a messenger from Rome. He has news that two battalions are on the way to Hippo. It is true: the whole of North Africa is under siege. The Vandals have swept down on the outposts and destroyed them. Now the larger cities are at stake. They surround them, let supplies and morale dwindle, and then attack. All the people of Hippo need do is wait. It is only a matter of time.

Hundreds of chickens lie dead in the streets. Their heads have been chewed off. Cows stand moaning, bleeding, mouth-sized wounds in their flanks. Horses, eyes rolling wildly, lie on their sides, their forelegs missing.

Una broods, paces the small room in the tower and broods.
—Crapulent, she complains. Crapulent crapulent crapulent.
—Excuse me?
Augustine raises his head from his writing.
—You heard me, Hairy Mac.
—For instance?
—The world. Out there. You know.
—I don't know.
—You do.

YELLOW

—I don't.

—Need I list?

—By all means.

—Barbarians! Rape and mutilation and disease! Paranoia knocking on the trap-door! Dead cows and dead chickens and salty water! . . .

Una was on a roll.

Augustine grinned.

—The loss of good has been given the name *evil*, Sucky Moll my dear.

—Well, there's a hell of a lot of goodlessness then.

—Where? Here? In the straw of our bed? In the papers on my desk? In this pear?

—You know damn well where I mean. Don't go philosophical on me.

—What?

—Bull.

—Bull?

—Shit.

—Nonsense. You want to be happy, be happy. You want to be sad, be sad.

—Coronary thrombosis. Cancer. Liver malfunction. Cataracts. Arthritis. Sciatica. Degenerating joints. Bad feet. Stolen wash. Broken wheels. Beat-up kids . . . Need I go on?

—Sucky Moll, Sucky Moll. That's out *there*. *Out there*. In *here* there are flatulation competitions, jokes, merriment. Making love. What is better than making love? In here everything is fine, Sucky Moll. Your bruises bespeak that.

—Optimist.

—Don't go using that sort of language with me.

—Optimist optimist optimist.

—You're losing it, Sucky Moll. Get a hold on yourself.

—I don't want to get a hold on myself.

—And anyway, there are worse things in the world than optimists.

—Optimist.

Augustine has left his desk, and is stalking. He makes a weak plunge, she a youthful sprint, and the theologian tumbles and thumps into straw. He straightens himself out and pats the place next to him.

—Come *on*, he tempts.

Una pouts.

—I don't feel like it.

—Sucky Moll-oll, he croons.

Una pouts.

—Come on, Sucky.

Una pouts, but less and less.

Augustine makes a grimace, grabs his ankles, pulls his legs over his head, and rocks.

—*Pft!* he goes.

Una smiles.

—*Poof!* he goes.

And Una giggles.

—*Brrrrrrrrrrrupupupupupupupupup!* he goes.

And Una laughs. She laughs and laughs and laughs.

A screaming drifts across the still morning. Another follows. Suddenly there is a scrambling in the street below, and the scrape of wheels on pavement, and the abrupt clatter of hooves, and a woman's wail. A great rumble tumbles down the avenues and Augustine wakes up completely aware, a tight fist grabbing his heart, staring at Una, who is already at the window, lemon light clinging to her like a mist, brown hair falling over her naked shoulders, breasts sagging, a hot wind in the room. A blast reverberates through the streets, the echo of the gates crashing in. And already Augustine has reached the trapdoor, has bolted it, has rolled the bed over it, is standing next to Una at the window (pink puffiness of her face; dullness in her eyes; quiver of the tiny muscles below her left temple, by the mole), his arm around her, watching the beautiful fires

yellow

throughout Hippo; watching the fat smoke-columns churning; hearing the bells tolling madly, the amazed shrieks, the howls of the pig-nosed barbarians as they stampede and snap like dogs at the sky. Already the door below the couple has crashed in. Already the thumping of feet booms, and shoulders are smashing against clay walls, and clubs are pounding, tables toppling, pottery splintering. Already footfalls on the ladder, the clump of angry sticks on the trapdoor, and Augustine is stepping back, his mouth open, his eyes raised, his palms cupped over his ears, and Una is shouting and crying at the same time, *Come back here, you bastard! Come back!* and Augustine *I can't help it, I can't stop it* and that is true, he is rising, he is rising off the floor in the attic of some tower in Hippo, he is dissolving into a fog of white light as the trapdoor bursts and the bed upturns and the tiny room is aflutter in a cloud of white doves, a marvelous cloud flickering with white doves.

BECAUSE I AM TACTFUL AND LEWD

Rick Kempa

(X Ranch, Idaho)

In Grandma's basement, let's fuck
on something that doesn't squeak,

cuz she's not snoring like she'd
snore if she weren't listening.

(Grandpa we won't think about.
Even if I hollered when we

came instead of biting at
the pillow Grandma made, he

wouldn't dismount from his dreams.)
When we don't go to town with them

to eat prime rib, I'll holler until
the horses bolt, and the hawks kick

the fattest chick out of the nest,
and the brahma bull comes bawling

home, and the greyhounds leave the cats
alone, and the mice spill out of

the loaves of hay, and the wind blows
and blows and blows us all away.

yellow

LOVESONG

■

Mikhail Horowitz

I joy in yr fingers,
thrilling in the gristmill
of yr tickling, & oh
yr callosities, & the tender
antennae extending
yr skin, seethrough skin
as fine as old rice-
paper, & don't I love
to nuzzle against yr breasts,
to muscle up & softly
rub yr udders, to
glory in yr dorsal
fin to titillate
yr tusks, to be marooned
& lazy in yr mane,
to stroke yr claws to
kiss you in the quills,
to dance w/you an
antler-jag, a knockabout
foxtrot, snout-to-
snout, to
howl & keen & shout &
screech, to squawk
each bird, each burrowing
creature out

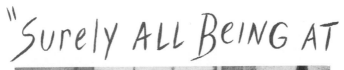

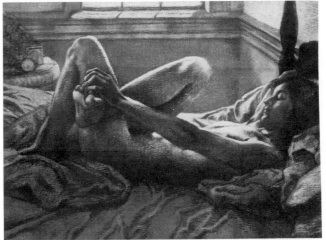

PERCOLATION

■

*Jane
Hirshfield*

In this rain that keeps us inside,
the frog,
wisest of creatures
to whom all things come,
is happy, rasping out of himself
the tuneless anthem of Frog.
Further off and more like ourselves
the cows are raising a huddling protest,
a rag-tag crowd, that can't get its chanting in time.
Now the crickets,
seeming to welcome the early-come twilight,
come in: of all orchestras, the most plaintive.
Still, in this rain soft as fog
that can only be known to be rain by the windows' streaming,
surely all Being at bottom is happy—
soaked to the bone, sopped at the root,
fenny, seeped through, yielding as coffee grounds
yield to their percolation, blushing, completely seduced,
assenting as they give in to the downrushing water,
the murmur of falling, the fluvial, purling wash
of all the ways matter loves matter:
riding its gravity down, into the body,
rising through cell-strands of xylem, leaflet and lung-flower,
back into air.

yellow

THE MOON IN RICE WINE

■

Lily Pond

My name is John Barstow Lewellen III, but my friends call me Jack. Or else they call me "Old Snort." I don't know why they call me that—I'm not old and I don't snort, unless you count the sound I make when I sit down too hard—something like a horse, I guess. It's not funny, see, I've gotten kind of big the last few years, well, fat, really, like, you know, where you kind of hate going out of the house sometimes.

Oh, I still go out but it's not the same; I used to go everywhere. Beautiful women were my specialty: their little freckled arms with all that wet curly blond hair under them, those breasts for resting . . . but you know, after a while. Oh, I don't know, maybe I'm too sensitive—I am, you know. Should have been born a girl—I always knew that; sometimes when I wake up in the morning I can't remember if I'm a guy or a girl, if you can believe that.

Anyway, after a while, like I was saying, you know, all those necks, wrists; I wanted one neck, my own personal set of wrists for Chrissakes. That's another thing: I read too much—I even sound like goddamned Holden Caulfield (and what a heavy name *that* is, if you think about it). What I really should be is a poet. Not like Rod McKuen or anything, but something important. I don't know; maybe then I could stop all this crazy . . . anyway . . . like I was saying. . . .

I had to stop seeing all these women. Depressed the hell out of me. Then I'm sitting around the house all the time, not knowing what to do with myself. You know how it is—you start getting lazy: you order out a lot for pizza, Chinese food. You start eating a lot of food that's "simple": French bread, thick steaks (you know, where the outside is nice and black and the inside is dripping with little beads of blood and . . .) . . . ah, well . . . anyway . . . here I am. Or here I was, until I met the Chinese chick.

SILK

I mean this chick was a goddamned dream; if that guy Botticelli had been Oriental, man, he would have for sure painted her rising right out of the ocean on a big half-shell, all her black hair flying, little apricot angels all around her. Scared the shit out of me.

It was like this, see: I was hanging out at Moe's bookstore, you know, the back room, where they have the *used* books; it was summer, almost night, muggy. The fans were going, Vivaldi on the radio. I walked in and joined all the other sad-looking guys with nothing better to do who were lying all over the floor, sitting on little step stools, or just leaning up against the cases.

I checked out a few things: Kosinski, Nabokov, before I got myself immersed in Thomas Mann, I think it was, yes, I remember: "In this pathos, this obligation, this reverence of man for himself, is God; in a hundred milliards of Milky Ways I cannot find him." I needed somebody's dreams.

So I'm standing there, one hand in my pants pocket playing with my keys, and the other with one finger propping open a blue, hardcover copy of *Doctor Faustus*, when I look up and she is standing right across from me barefooted. In a yellow satin coat.

And she's staring right at me. But then she pretends not to be, and starts moving to the music from the radio over towards the poetry. I could smell her from there: like a thousand purple flowers; I smelled like a goddamned raincoat. My face began to split apart.

I tried putting the book away and suddenly my hands were like pale heavy birds flying laboriously up to the shelf. The mystery and glory of the books around me, there only a moment ago, had died. I was a man with heavy testicles hanging from a loose middle; that cobra-baby, mother-of-pearl, shock of a girl terrified me. I had to get out of there.

I find him like a small snake; white bellied; his slime is fascinating me; he will scurry back beneath the rock; he will scream if cornered.

yellow

The street smelled like a goddamned ashtray before a rain: little relief. It was like the girl, that quickly, had put my spirit in her pocket—gone, clean gone, like the last line of coke, gone. With barely an echo around the corner.

And yet from right at first I feel him in my hair; a covenant in lava; he is in my skin before he even knows it; it begins; I feel his grimy face beside my cheek hours ahead of time; my lizard.

I started walking. I walked up the street. I walked down the damned street, so I swear I knew the fact that she was following me was no accident. I couldn't stand it; I could feel the blackheads in my nose. Then she passes me and goes on down the street. I couldn't believe it, how I was so enormously relieved. I followed her down the street.

Now, there's this little Soup Kitchen on the corner and, well, I always eat there anyway, so I can say I might have gone in there whether she had or not, but, like I said, she did. There was a wind coming up—it might have rained; I went in too. I sat down at one old table, not too far from her, and spent a lot of time staring at the menu.

The next thing, I swear, I don't know how she did it, but she made me talk to her. I said something stupid like, "Did you ever eat here before?"

She answers me. I mean, like her eyes answer me before she does, tricky. Then she says, "I have eaten here many times." She smiles.

I get bold. "I can't decide what to get." Very stupid thing to say but apparently she doesn't think so because she keeps talking to me.

"Yes, it is all very good." Another smile. Already, of course, I am ready to wash her feet with my best clothes just for carrying on this half-assed conversation with me. Like a pure donkey brain I ask, "What do you recommend?"

"I will take noodle soup and some peach ice cream."

"Oh! That sounds great! Mind if I join you?"

Now I'm grinning like a goddamned horse-jockey on top of

the line and she's stopped, but she holds out her chair for me so, hey, I sit down.

The chick tells me her name is Chinese Rose Arlene, if you can believe that. I tell her they call me Jack; I don't mention the "Old Snort" part. I don't mention much of anything, just sit there eating the goddamned weirdest dinner I ever had and not noticing a goddamned thing but the way her little straight eyelashes fall down and up over her black eyes; her skin is the color of honey with cream in it, her nostrils look softer than a baby's ear. Her wrists.

And then she stands up like a gladiola blossoming and says she needs a ride home.

So we're standing at my car, one nine six four Dodge Dart, piece of shit, not really, whole goddamn car a dung pile of half-rotted taco chips and Jack-in-the-Box cartons; I'm thinking, like, what a mess . . . I should have cleaned this car six months ago . . . , and then she says, right out of the blue, like she's reading my mind or something, "It doesn't matter."

And if that doesn't blow me away enough right there, we're driving up towards her house and she says, eyelids half-lowered, she hasn't looked at me since we got in the car, "You have been feeling uncomfortable lately." Not even a question, just says it. I go to say something and she takes this tiny little breath and says, "When we get to my house, you will allow me to tell your fortune?" This is a question and I haven't any answer. Up Dwight Way into the darkness.

At his car, I feel I am falling through him like a funnel. I will read his stones when we are at my house; I tell him; he has always been there; in the restaurant, in his car, I could hear him; I did not know what I would hear; if I had, perhaps I would not have listened.

She leads me up these little, overgrown steps alongside her house to her backyard and even though my feet feel about seven sizes too big, I'm following her like a rat to a Hamlin tune, with my eyes fixed up past her on the dark sky with its moon hanging there like a gigantic nipple, and it makes me

yellow

want to howl like the goddamned dachshund I had when I was six years old. She tells me to go sit down and already I'm turned insideout by her like a wet glove so I do what she says. She disappears.

I sit there in a cool breeze; dark, hilly, starlit. Waiting. The grass smells freshcut, and there's crickets. She returns, bringing me a cup of wine. By the smell, it's rice wine. I can't look at her so I look into the cup; the moon is reflected on the surface of the wine.

After he drinks, he is looser, like silk-moths. He thinks he hides in his fat but I see him. When he talks, his voice is not like his spirit.

"So how you gonna tell my fortune?"

I lead him into my kitchen; my answer will be slower than the night in welcoming him.

I've never seen anything like this chick's kitchen: a temple to her. She's got lace everywhere, and jars of roses; red brocade banners from the ceiling, green glass circles hanging in the dark windows, bunches of dried leaves. I am sucked into her magic.

She lights a purple candle on the table and reaches into her skirt to pull out a satchel pulled with a string at the top. She opens it and eight round black stones drop out onto the table. She studies them, and the world stops.

"You are returning home after a long absence."

I look to see where she sees this but the stones all look the same to me; I feel a strange pressure starting like a snake tightening itself around my head. "Where do you see that?" She doesn't answer directly, but begins to speak.

"You have not known happiness for a long time; you have been in the walled city, looking for a way out." She pauses, then the words flow out of her. "Stuck behind the looking glass, the red rivers your hair. Ducks eating everything before it has a chance to grow; the ears of corn infested by worms."

I look at her, Are you reading my fortune or telling my dreams?

She looks at me in wonder like a schoolgirl, I do not know.

"A woman in the cave, only a fire for warmth; the crane is singing, robbing your heart of its beat . . ."

My words are coming from a place I do not know; I hear them; my voice is speaking and I am lost in it.

In a swift whirl of wind I feel us tango across her red brocade; I was being caressed by the long arms of universal law and order. I tried to listen; her images spun around me like birds in an Alfred Hitchcock flick.

"Your hands are so dirty." I look up at the catch in her voice and there's this one billowing tear spilling off her eyelid creasing the yellow velvet of her cheek; my hand would not let it fall; my thumb caught it.

I need now his hand in mine; to cleanse it; with tears; the dragons were calling; their green song; parades in the town; the tide encased me; his hand in mine; my hands are no longer brown; they are scaly; and they are not my own.

She gives me back my hand and it is clean but it is without her; the molecules of air in the room seem to compress into small knots around us and then disperse as her voice comes back like a shadow across the water: "In a pomegranate there are many seeds, each with a sweet juice of its own. They do not touch each other until the fruit is rolled and bruised, and the thin shell of each seed is broken, and the juices run together." She has stopped looking at the stones and is staring into the night.

The stones are talking for themselves. Have I cried for this man? I am demolished; I am bud burst into bloom.

What are you doing to me?

I don't know.

"And like the pomegranate, the parts inside of you do not move in harmony, so you do not know they are there, but I see Persian kings and Balinese dancers, fresh running water and deer on the hill, birds in the doorway, and music from pipers . . ."

I did not want to become you; I did not want to become you; I

yellow

held on; we were bees in the same hive; we were fleas; we were drag-
ons; flaming; is this not my kitchen; my table; wooden?

What is happening?

I don't know.

I don't know.

I . . .

I . . .

and then in a moment a lightswitch seemed to go on which
didn't make it lighter . . . just . . . changed everything. I
flashed on an Escher drawing: "Bond of Union"—a man's and a
woman's heads formed, both of them, of one continuous
Moebius strip, space in them, space out of them, in an infinite
spiral of endless . . .

She stood up dropping the stones.

I know only to enter my brown room and remove my clothing;
this merging I understand. The man understands also.

When I drop to sleep from him I fall into a large camellia.

You know how you feel in the morning? Like there's hardly any stars left so you know the night's gone by, but you feel
a little weird because you didn't get much of any sleep and everything's a little warped; but, man, just watching her, soft and
gentle on her pillow, black and brown and smooth on her white
pillow, I wanted to fill myself with her as much as I'd filled
her with me so many times the night before. She might never
want to see me again.

She turns and hums, a small pocket of a hum; I should
have said something sweet, I know that, a single sweet word or
something—hi, honey—but, like, my stomach rocks up and I
feel my fingers getting all tense again. I try not looking straight
at her, locking my teeth which are all dried up, "Uh, you want
to get together again sometime?" Jesus, what a stupid question.

"You collect worrying like a packrat."

"What do you mean? I didn't say anything! . . ." Shit!
Why did I say that? Now she'll start hating me . . . just like
every other goddamned chick I ever met . . . I never should

have followed her . . . they're all alike . . . I should have stayed in that goddamned bookstore and . . .

"Stop," she said.

"Stop!" she said fiercely.

She looked at me, without her wings, her roses, her fragrance, or her moisture. She looked into my eyes from one bare bone to another and her voice was hard and hollow. "You can manage."

Somehow, her words went down my throat and filled me the way food and lazy kissing never had; I was shocked and filled and suddenly felt like laughing! I didn't question the door slamming inside of me and the new one opening. I just put my arms around her and lifted her skinny body out of her bed, out of her white sleep, into the blue morning, and in my arms I twirled her around in her room and I laughed and she laughed and we laughed. And laughed.

yellow

That winter we took turns stepping into
the barely started mornings to turn ignitions
until they caught, complaining roughly
of the cold, then ran
back to finish our coffee, cereal, toast,
while, chokes pulled full out,
exhaust poured white across the glass
that kept us warm . . .
We'd named them: Big Mama Tomato, Snooze.
Each was our first, as we
were each other's first, in the farmhouse
for rent for the first time
in forty years surrounded by soybeans.
We'd whited-over the pink room the son
had painted when he returned crazed with Vietnam.
We'd made the man come back for the thin black lab
left chained in the yard.
The thirteen cats stayed, soon more, all wild.
Our own would come to the window by way of
a three-story oak and moss-shingled porch roof,
to mew us awake and them in every day:
Kesey & Mountain Girl, scrawling their signatures
snow-mornings on the quilt.
We nailed planks from the old barns onto the walls
by our bed, scraped a dozen layers of peeling paper
from the next room—the older they got,
the more lovely. That one we made cheerful yellow,
where I wrote the wildly sad poems of the very young.
When we got to the farm you took a tractor, I loaded

my van with sacks of produce & drove off.
Kip supervised us all: the Peace Corps vet, the kids
just out of school. Picking his peaches that summer
the best work I've done, the closest to Paradise
I've seen, ladder-propped in his trees.
All sold now, gone, his farm, the one we lived at,
the groundfall cider, the cars.
Us too, of course, long shaken free, though
I still cook bluefish the way you taught me, and carrots.
I thought I would love you forever—and, a little, I may,
in the way I still move towards a crate, knees bent,
or reach for a man: as one might stretch
for the three or four fruits that lie in the sun at the top
of the tree; too ripe for any moment but this,
they open their skin at first touch, yielding sweetness,
sweetness and heat, and in me, each time since,
the answering yes.

"O ANN'S FOR THE

rAIN TO TAKE"

THEN

■

*Marilyn
Hacker*

I was due home at seven, and you were
staying downtown. We shared a premature
glass of white wine.

           "I'll walk you downstairs."

                                              "Sure."

Out on the dim landing, you pushed the door
shut behind us, one hand on the small
of my back, then pushed me back against the wall
hung with winter coats. I almost slipped
in the half-dark; half-gasped as you unzipped
my pants and tugged them down, silencing my
exclamation with your tongue, your thigh
opened mine. I grabbed your ass with one
hand, hair with the other. You began
stroking my belly, but I pulled you close
against me, covering what you'd exposed.
You whispered, "Should I get down on my knees
and lick you?"

                "No, with your hand, like that, there, please!"
Mouth on your mouth, I rode you, barely stand-
ing up, or standing it. You moved your hand
past where I put it, through the parting, wet
for you already, spread me, and I let
you deep in, while your lips went soft beneath
my mouth, and I tasted salt behind your teeth.
Your fingers brought the juices down around
what swelled into your palm, until you found
where it would come from. Inches of my bare

yellew

skin burned against your jeans. Into your hair
I pleaded, "Let me," but you wouldn't; pulled
a centimeter back, instead. The chill
air on my skin pulsed through me like a smack,
and, for a breath, I let my head fall back
against the linen sleeves and woolen folds,
then drew you onto me, so I could hold
myself up to your kisses, while you took
me, out and in, with your whole hand. I shook,
off balance, needed it, you, just there. I
thrust up against you. Then my inner thigh
muscles convulsed, and I bore down on you,
wrenching out "Now!" as heat arrowed into
the place you had me, till I couldn't stop
it coming, crushed against you, half on top
of you, or you on me, breathed through your lips
a huge, collapsing sigh. Arms round my hips,
holding my ass, you kissed me as I hung
on your shoulders, prodded my hair back with your tongue.
You covered me till I recovered my
balance, and my butt, to say, "Good-bye."
"Call you later."
                    "Ummm." Buttoned, I pushed
away, blinking, stepped back. "I've got to rush!"
and watched my footing down three rickety
flights toward twilight traffic in Chelsea.

SILK

SATURDAY MORNING

■

*Marilyn
Hacker*

While you sleep off the brandy, little one
my hand could find its way back to the place
it knows so well, now. Even with your face
turned away from me, sleeping in till noon,
you move right through me. After we were done
talking (thence the brandy) until four
AM, you, in the dark, played three songs for
me while I dozed—so tired I couldn't come
when you'd tried for me. So you sat on the floor
with the guitar, beside me, troubador,
and then, naked, you woke me to you, brought me
down on your mouth, brought it down and caught me
in the grey dawn, whose sunburst was your name
like brandy in my throat as I came and came.

yellow

CITY OF MEN

■

Donald Rawley

I am in love in a city of men.

Men who grab
my backward glance
with the threatened beat
of their breath,
men whose nights
are convenient and sly.
Men with mirrored glasses and rifles
laughing on the freeway,
men who punch the air with
their angry sex,
men with the squint of a hyena.

This is my city
and I smoke cigarettes like convicts.

My men are as peerless as dukes
with the static strength of statues,
with their cocks in hand
tempting fate
and the hair on their bellies a warning.
My men are prudent with joy,
men who discard love and memory
when their sight
has big muscle and hair.
Men who allow me crime and melancholy.
Men who allow me nothing.
I take it all like barbiturates
and I am in a sleep of men.
Men who disorient me.

They take my eyes like dice.
I study their buttocks with
the greed of a child.

Men. I can be a vanishing act.

Men who know how to smoke a cigarette
without women's fingers,
men who understand their role.
Men with caked hair
under their arms,
men with pink skin and a lisp,
beautiful men with histories and gifts
as constant as a fine bell.
Men who die for no reason.
Men who have a white light,
like Valentino or Clara Bow,
the light moths
kill themselves for,
the white light that makes me
sit up and blink like a child,
a pupil
a student of men's eyes
lit with candles and starch,
a congregation of men
who are fireflies and saints.

Men who are as kind as
any animal who can steal.
As kind as your sexual history of Mexico
with your men reeling with tequila.
Men who smell fine as dirt
and the salty perfume of paid sex,
men who allow their semen
to run through every channel.

Men. I can touch their palms when I dream.

Yellow

■

Young men with still perfect limbs,
ex-husbands in loud sweaters,
groomed men with clenched teeth
who hover in packs
beyond the shotgun eyes
of deserted women,
fat men with a comic's sweat and ripe hands,
tired men sitting on safe settees
full of bibles and loss
beyond the dull swipe
of rolled lawns,
men who make love with piety
canonized in a frenzy of flesh,
men who masturbate their lives
so that even daylight
becomes their own private keyhole.

Men with cars for girlfriends,
men who live in air-conditioned ruins
choking with ghosts and fearing rain,
men who slam doors and telephones,
men who have secrets and money
and clean nails,
black men with skin
like wet grapes
and teeth like winter clouds,
drunk men who walk like dancing bears,
old men with wrinkled, ruined cocks
that peek out like rummy sailors,
men whose skin accumulates layers
like a granite shelf,
men with twisted veins like
Monterey pines running down
their clenched arms and spread legs.

SILK

■

Men whose lust is hurried and benign,
men whose lips are a crime,
men who are boys that play
with black leather and Vaseline,
boys who shadow box their
fancy passions in alleys
and steam rooms until dawn.
Men who ride horses naked in the desert.
Men who surrender nothing.

Men with the pinched faces of thin air,
staring out of glass buildings
so high they can only see mountains
they do not understand.
Men in average blue suits
with wives in another state,
men with the laughter of poets
running elevators and pumping gas
with delicious, cracked large dry lips,
smoking unfiltered Pall Malls
and scratching their asses.

These are the men with the rhythm of
my city's white light,
men whose eyes are lit by gin and possibilities,
men who work in airports
and have never flown,
men who are not safe in numbers,
men who drive beat-up cars
and live with scarred women,
men who watch the stars
with drugs and candles
from the roofs of shabby buildings,
men who come like a car wreck,

Yellow

■

men who are mindless
with prodigy,
men who eat rocks,
men with cypress green eyes
and hairy shoulders,
men who devour
a callous embrace,
all the men I find
beyond my barricades,
all men that tell me
of hymns of earth
and the strength of my loins,
of tasting the white light,
of being in love in a city of men.

AT THE CINEMA

(AFTER FERNANDO ARRABAL)

■

David Fisher

We were at the cinema, the two of us.
Instead of watching the film I
watched her. I touched her earrings and
smoothed her lashes. Then I kissed
her knees and put on her lap a
paper hat that I made with the tickets!

She watched the film and laughed.
Then I caressed her bosom and
each time I pressed one of her
breasts, a blue fish came out . . . . !

yellow

ANN

■

*David
Fisher*

Ann came for apples.
I died all day.
I went between her blossoms
              like a ram.

The children are like her,
              (Pretty-bones) and
                            (Meadow-shape)

In her youth
Ann picks apples—and is restless.
She desires
another joy, a farther moon . . .
Sometimes at night
Sometimes at night
I hear her humming as she learns.

Her hair is raven black, she's near
the sweet white heart of the grass.
She and her children are three cool peaches
in a white split basket.

See, she has swaddled the children up
                      like little firs/

o ann's for the rain to take.

"IT WAS
SIMPLY A

MATTER OF
PAYING
ATTENTION"

THE THANATOTIC PREJUDICE

■

Mary Mackey

When you teach literature in America, you teach death. I have here beside me a typical introductory text which of course contains *Death in Venice* and *The Death of Ivan Ilyich*, not to mention *Noon Wine* (double murder, suicide) and *A Rose for Emily* (necrophilia).

From time to time my students ask me why great literature is so gloomy. They inquire nervously if you have to commit suicide to be a real poet, and exactly what it was Shelley was so upset about. I am forced to tell them the truth: that only death is taken seriously in our culture; that only death is honored and extolled as a fit topic for our greatest writers. The comic and erotic are trivial, sidelights, fit only for TV sitcoms, nightclubs, and bar napkins.

I exaggerate, of course. After all, we do have Vonnegut, Irving, Piercy, and Harris. But I submit to you that the dominant tone of what we revere as great literature is crepuscular. I call this exclusive veneration of death-in-art the thanatotic prejudice.

Now, I would be the last person to argue that death is trivial or uninteresting. It is one of the great borderlines of human experience, beyond which strange lands or cold nothings may stretch. As far as we know, we cannot touch, manipulate, or move the dead, and our hatreds, loves, greeds, and passions are probably matters of indifference to them. Thus death is a natural resolution to the problem of plot, a kind of automatic end to the karmic complications of a novel, poem, play, or short story.

But the great lyric triad has always included love and nature as well as death. Once we grant that death is well taken care of, we must ask why we are so short on nature and love at present.

Now, thanatos is the opposite of eros; like the Hindu gods

yellow

Shiva and Brahma, the first moves toward dissolution and the second toward creation. In most other cultures, and at many other times in our own history, this balance has been carefully preserved. Stone-age tribes in Colombia bury their dead in the fetal position in womb-shaped jars; the early gods of Nepal copulate with skulls in their hands and dance the dance of creation on a pile of bones; Greek actors in goat skins thwack one another with six-foot-long stuffed phalli and tell off-color jokes in honor of Dionysus; Romeo calls death amorous and asks if it has taken Juliet for a bride; at my great-uncle's Irish wake the mourners drink, dance, and sing bawdy ballads. Life thrives in the presence of death; at birth we die into life. Creation leads to dissolution, dissolution to creation.

But the thanatotic prejudice breaks this primal balance, uproots and denigrates the erotic, discards the living flesh of art, leaving only the skeleton behind. Instead of the seductive we are left with the pornographic: fold-out bunnies, blowup party dolls. A survey is taken of Americans and we discover that over 70 percent of us would be willing to date (and even marry) robots if suitable imitations could be produced. We tell the poll takers that we have given up on human relationships. We want mates we can recharge like cassette recorders, programmed to be faithful, unfailingly amorous, and warranted to run for sixty years without back talk. We want life and art to assume a certain pose and never move from it, forgetting that the only unmoving things are dead.

Hence most of pornography is not erotic; it is thanatotic, anti-sex propaganda. Like the Puritan, the pornographer believes in his heart that sex is wicked, and so he recreates it as a violent attack where rape replaces courtship, where there is no conception or birth, only dominance, suffering, and death.

Elsewhere the same theme prevails, teaching us that only death is real, only death worthy of respect. The thanatotic prejudice encourages us to believe that plans for stockpiling nuclear weapons are somehow more serious, more mature than our childish, trivial plans for peace and disarmanent.

We do in the streets, courts, and congresses of our country what we dream in our poems. Art is the cutting edge of the soul. When societies change and civilizations fall, the warning signs appear first in the architecture, the frescoes, the myths and popular songs.

When a culture stops respecting the erotic, it proclaims to the world that it has chosen a particular path, one that leads away from life. As far as I can see, that path can have only one end.

yellow

I am my body. And my body is dead, thought Estelle Greenhouse. "What a hoot," Estelle giggled silently, realizing that she could still laugh even though she could see that her jaws were locked in that same tight grimace she had always made whenever Eli had surprised her from behind by suddenly cupping his hands around her gigantic, Maidenform-encased breasts, when she was vacuuming for instance. Her breasts looked huge to Estelle as they lay unmoving, no longer heaving up and down in time with her breathing. At least she no longer had to worry about that squishing sound they made, which Estelle had always suspected that everyone could hear. Now, her breasts were like two twin peaks, the nipples erect and looking almost perky through the hospital gown her body was wearing. "Hmm, I wonder if they get hard like that when everyone dies," Estelle asked herself. What if people saw them and thought she had died while thinking about sex?

Well, not worth the worry. Eli would surely have her dressed in that royal blue velvet gown she had bought two months ago at Saks. Her nipples wouldn't show through that fabric, she reassured herself, as she imagined all her friends and relatives, probably even that bitch sister of hers, Lucille, admiring her in the new dress. She hoped that Eli would remember to bring those satin pumps she had dyed to match. "Above all, dear God," Estelle prayed, "please let Eli insist that Pierre does my hair for the funeral instead of some nimcombob undertaker's assistant." After all, she wanted to knock their socks off. Estelle had always loved her body and now that it was dead, the love seemed to be growing even stronger every second.

Estelle had always assumed that, like most women, she would outlive her husband, Eli, and after a year or two of deep mourning, she would move permanently to their Palm Beach condo tax shelter where she would spend her days playing mah jongg with the other widows and the evenings at the adult education classes at the local high school. Even in New Rochelle, Estelle had never tired of learning and continuously signed up for such courses as "Heroines in Literature," "Chinese Vegetarian Cooking," and "Macramé Plant Hangers," depending on what was popular that semester. Estelle had a thirst for knowledge, Eli liked to say, pointing to her with pride at one of the dinners he was always hosting for visiting representatives of his firm's international branches. And yet, here she was dead. She was definitely not breathing. Estelle floated down to make a final check and somehow she knew that this wasn't just some nightmare.

Now what? Do I just hang around my body till it gets buried, Estelle wondered impatiently, but suddenly happy that she hadn't opted for the pre-planned cremation package that was all the rage with her friends. It certainly would be eerie to watch her body lit on fire like one of those Buddhist anti-war monks and to see it bubble, melt, and turn dry and crackly into gray ash and pieces of burnt-to-a-crisp bones. Ever since her course on "The Holocaust—Never Again!" at Temple Beth-El, Estelle had no longer considered cremation as a possibility. Just to be sure, she had asked Eli to promise to put her in a moisture-proofed mausoleum. "No worms or maggots, thank you. It may be denial," she had argued with him, "but I have absolutely no interest in mouldering away for years fertilizing the cemetery's lawn."

So where were the bright lights, the humming noise, the tunnel, the line-up of previously dead relatives ready to welcome her with open arms? Estelle had, of course, read *Life After Life* by Dr. Moody for her course on "Death and Dying—The Five Stages and Beyond," and she was expecting certain things to happen. Where was Uncle Harry in his shiny grass green suit slapping her too hard on her back and saying, "Welcome,

yellow

my honeypie. Nothing to worry about up here. The food is great, all-you-can-eat buffets at every meal. You sure are looking lovely. Never seen you look so cute, Estellie." And he would pinch her cheeks with his fat, stubby fingers, vaguely hurting her. And Grandma Nettie, dressed in her frayed pink chenille robe and fake fur slippers. "Oy vey iz mir," she'd say, "if it isn't my precious Stella D'Oro cookie come to join us. Come closer, mine eyes are not so good no more. Cataracts." And after a big hug, Nettie would laugh and cry at the very same time. "Oy, how I've missed my favorite little girl. Don't worry nothing, Nana will take good care of you. You be okay-dokey in my hands." And even Anna May, her childhood maid, black as burning coal in the shiny, otherworldly light, would be there to greet her, saying, "Miss Estelly! Remember when we hid your cat from your mamma that day she was gonna give it to the ASPCA? We sure bamboozled her, didn't we? I sure wished I'd lived to see you growing up, sugar, but, my, my, my, you look like quite the fancy lady. I sure is proud of you, Miss Est-telly."

But so far no familiar visions had appeared, no lights, nothing. Estelle was just hanging out near the hospital room ceiling. She still held some hope that there would be something more to death; but, at the same time, she hoped that it wouldn't turn out to be too scary. She especially hoped that the Catholics were wrong about sins and hell. Estelle hated the feel of even a mild sunburn and the vision of burning for eternity had always terrified her more than cremation, even though she was Jewish and wasn't supposed to believe in such things. "So far, so good," Estelle reassured herself, as no devil had arrived in the vicinity. She had, after all, shoplifted as a teenager and masturbated quite a few times over the years, and Estelle seemed to remember that these were supposed to be mortal sins. But worst of all, she had once let her neighbor Josh Shulman, who was married and was Eli's best friend, feel her up at a party.

SILK

And she hadn't been really drunk, just mildly high on the wine punch. Estelle shivered pleasantly as she pictured Josh's fingers circling slowly up her slightly sticky thighs until he parted them and stuck his pointing finger right up under the elastic legband of her bodysuit and began to twirl her pubic hairs until they heard Eli's voice calling her from another room. Josh quickly extricated his moist finger and the panty leg snapped, leaving a tiny but unmistakable bruise that Estelle had touched for several days afterward. Not that Eli wasn't great in bed. He was terrific. But the thought of Josh's finger still gave her a thrill she couldn't or wouldn't dare explain to anyone except her closest friend Sylvia, who was shocked but supportive. Just remembering this incident caused Estelle's clitoris to swell and throb tantalizingly until she realized again where she was and that she was dead and floating around without a real flesh-and-blood body. And yet she was absolutely positive she could feel juices rushing into her pussy.

How could she feel sexy now? Wasn't it some perversion like necrophilia, Estelle worried, as she felt an uncontrollable urge to play with herself. She wasn't sure how to do it at first—she could still see her body resting stiffly on the bed below—but there was no mistaking it, Estelle felt that familiar itch and the slow building up to a crescendo of tingling until she could feel her entire vagina, or where a vagina should be, start to vibrate and contract. "Ummmmm," she sighed, fantasizing Josh's finger rhythmically tweaking her most private part, as she allowed herself to have her first orgasm after death. It wasn't better, but it certainly wasn't worse or even much different. Perhaps death itself, its importance, had been grossly exaggerated by human beings. Apart from her ability to float, nothing much had changed so far. "Not a bad way to begin being dead," Estelle mused, and for a few minutes she rested in the afterglow. Like a miniature quartz heater, her clitoris sent out healing, relaxing waves of warmth. Suddenly she heard

yellow

Eli's familiar deep voice and Estelle felt herself blush with guilt and shame. How could she be thinking about, no less imagining Josh, when she had just died and left her dearly beloved husband Eli forever? At the very least, she should have been picturing Eli's penis pushing in and out; but somehow, after all those years together and even though she loved him as much as life itself, the image of his cute red-tipped wiener just made her smile. Damn it all, Eli just didn't inspire those pure lusty feelings she felt when Josh's fingers had parted her. "Oh God, there I go again," Estelle said to herself, stopping herself from thinking anymore about Josh. And she could see Eli quite clearly now, usually so calm and unemotional, he was sobbing as he held her waxy, lifeless hand. She could hear him pleading with her, "Estelle, I love you, my sweet darling. Don't leave me. Don't die. Please come back." She felt touched by his uncharacteristic display and began to cry. Well, not to actually produce salty tears, but to cry in the same way she had tickled her clit. It wasn't in her imagination and it wasn't in her body. Someplace, somewhere, something unknown had replaced the old Estelle and she just couldn't define it.

Estelle tried to tell Eli that she was okay and that he should just look up at the ceiling and he would see her, but he ignored her pleas. God, she loved him to death. In fact, she reflected, it was a real shame that he hadn't died too. Then they could still be together. The way it was now, Eli didn't acknowledge her presence, couldn't see or hear her. He just kept looking at the lump on the bed. Finally Eli got up and began to walk out of the room, looking so sad that Estelle couldn't resist giving him a big kiss on the top of his bald spot. But he just reached up afterwards to scratch the spot as though he had been bitten by a mosquito and he left. Estelle tried to follow him, but found that she was unable to go very far. Unnoticed until now, she saw a very thin silver thread attaching her new essence to her dead body. She tried to break the thread, but thin as it looked, it was as rigid as a steel pipe. So Estelle was stuck hovering over her hospital bed, and she began to feel pissed off. "I thought I'd be free in death at least. I certainly hope I won't have to spend eternity guarding my mausoleum," Estelle said to herself. For a few moments, she wasn't so sure if her decision against cremation had been such a wise one. "If this is all there is to death, isn't it a foolish waste of a soul," Estelle complained. "I was hoping for a rest, a time to just lay back and relax after the years of committee meetings, fund-raisers, banquets, traveling, shopping, Eli's boring office parties, and all my classes. But no, here I am like some goddam ghost. Oh my God, that's it, I'm a ghost! How trite." Estelle had never believed in ghosts, despite Sylvia's insistence that ESP, *Seth Speaks*, and Uri Geller the Israeli forkbender were for real. Estelle had always argued, "I'll wait until I see a ghost to believe in them," and now she was not only seeing one, she was one. So all those phoney-baloney psychics were on to something. Well, maybe she could contact Eli through a medium and let him know that she was all right, but the image of him dressed in his Perry Ellis suit and Burberry raincoat sitting in some dark seedy room with a wild-haired gypsy woman, waiting for a table to begin tapping, just made Estelle laugh.

While she was lost in these images of Eli, Estelle didn't notice the sudden apparition of a luminous man floating near her on the ceiling, so when he tapped Estelle on the shoulder, she gasped, "My God, you about scared me to death." Noticing her faux pas, she giggled girlishly and moved a little to get a better view of him. This must be the messenger of death, Estelle guessed, as she realized with a shock that he appeared to be completely nude. There was no way she could overlook his almost 14 kt. gold pubic hair curling around the fattest and the longest penis she had ever seen, and his testicles looked like those gorgeous crystal Christmas tree balls you could buy for a fortune at Tiffany's. His face resembled Michelangelo's David. Estelle turned away, feeling quite shy, but she realized at the

yellow

very same moment that she too was naked as the day she was born. Even if it were in this strange, airy-fairy spirit body way, Estelle couldn't help wondering what this creature was thinking about her new form. She peeked and thought she caught him peering at her firm breasts, but he quickly met her eyes. "So are you the big guy, yourself? Death?" Estelle asked a bit coquettishly. And with a voice that sounded like an entire orchestra made up of harps, flutes and violins, he replied, "Estelle, my precious soul, can't you see that there is no death? There's only love, formless and eternal. And I am part of the love which welcomes you to this new realm."

Estelle thought he sounded a bit like one of those crazy gurus she had heard at the New School and hoped that there wasn't some mistake. Had they forgotten she was Jewish and sent her to the wrong section? Apparently he could read her thoughts because immediately he said, "There are no dogmas here, no forms. Religions are meaningless when we are joined in love." Estelle wondered, blushing, if he also knew that she had noticed his gigantic cock but she tried to push those kinds of thoughts out of her mind as he seemed to have a philosophic bent and she figured that she better not screw things up. Certainly not now. But when she glanced back over at him she was amazed to see that his dong was huge and violet and pointing straight at her. He smiled and reached over to embrace Estelle, but she moved back. "I thought you said death was a place for formless love?" Estelle asked, feeling quite confused and very curious. "Ah, Estelle, you voluptuous spirit, there are no rules to love here, none at all," he replied while tweaking her left nipple with his long, elegant fingers.

"But, but . . . " Estelle sputtered, "I've never made love to anyone besides Eli, no less to a perfect stranger, and Eli and I have only been separated for a few hours at the most. He'd divorce me posthumously if he knew what I was up to. We've always been strictly monogamous." In spite of her protestations of fidelity, Estelle could feel her nipple turn into a pebble of delight as he continued rolling it back and forth, side to side. "On the other hand," she said to herself, "wasn't it Eli who always insisted, 'After one of us kicks the bucket and the other is left, the one who remains should have fun, date, maybe remarry, even. No need to sit home and grieve the rest of one's life away.' So even though it's me who's dead, I'm sure he'd want me to have a good time and do what I'm expected to do here, even though neither of us had any inkling that death was going to be anything like this." Estelle began to explain this to the stranger, saying, "If I had only known, I wouldn't have spent half my life being so scared about dying, so I suppose . . ." but she was interrupted by his raspberry lips pressing on hers and his soft, darting tongue probing deep into the caverns of her mouth. Estelle almost swooned. My Lord, she thought, he tastes so incredibly sweet, almost exactly like the gourmet version of Ambrosia Salad I used to make out of mandarin oranges, coconut, fresh pineapple chunks, real whipped cream and maple syrup. And the smell of his breath was just like inhaling the most expensive Belgian chocolates.

Estelle could feel him touching her all over and yet they were both like air. It was almost corny, and certainly nothing had ever prepared her for anything remotely like this. Maybe such knowledge was hidden in the secret Kabbalah she had heard mentioned for years, which only male Hebrew scholars were allowed to study. While considering this possibility, she heard him whisper, "Quiet your mind, Estelle. Let go of the past, the future, all those questions. Why, where, when, who. Just be here with me, in this moment. This instant, that's all there is," and with that she heard him laugh and felt his mouth begin to suck at her right breast, his tongue sliding round and round her areola and giving the cutest little flicks to her rock-hard nipple. Estelle began to moan and she felt the wetness between her legs begin to gush down and out between her pussy lips. Even that silly flirtation with Josh seemed like nothing

yellow

compared to the sensations she could feel traveling up and down her spine like a spreading fire. "To hell with inhibitions," Estelle cried out, as she reached down to grasp his dancing erection. It felt about the same as Eli's except her hands seemed to merge with it in a magical way she couldn't put into words. As she lifted his foreskin—the first she had ever seen—she reassured herself that it couldn't be unclean, certainly not here. Estelle felt a little liquid dribble delicately out of its tip, lubricating her fingers. As she moved her hand up and down the enormous shaft, she thought about her diaphragm and creams in her drawer at home, but she assumed that pregnancy was out of the question. "After all, you ninny," Estelle scolded herself, "nobody could give birth from a body that is dead. And postmenopausal, at that. Although, a child by him would be almost like Jesus." She started to picture herself in labor in a picturesque manger, when she heard him saying, "Come back, Estelle. Come with me and you'll give birth to yourself," and he stuck his pointing finger right into her creamy pleasure-hole, as Eli had always called it. He moved his finger much faster than her vibrator could go on its highest speed and soon Estelle began thrusting her hips up and down. God, how she wanted him, this stranger, this unknown creature of death, this ghost. She felt like fainting again, but fought it. Estelle wanted to stay conscious now for each and every scrumptious second.

Suddenly she felt a new sensation and looked up to see what it could be. Without having felt him move at all, he was now floating with his head resting in between her thighs and his luxurious tongue was lapping and licking at her pussy mouth in intricate figure-eights. It was divine. His mouth, his tongue and her cunt looked like one giant circle of light the color of tupelo honey and the air was even more fragrant than Joy, the world's most expensive perfume, which Eli had bought her on their past anniversary. Eli could never bring himself to do this to her, even though, as a treat once in awhile, Estelle would take his dick in her mouth. She would usually be able to hide the gagging as she swallowed his sperm, so she could understand his aversion to her down there. But now, Estelle regretted all those wasted years as she felt herself bathed in radiant rainbow hues while this angel's tongue slithered up and down her clitoris in a rhythm that was perfection. Without knowing how it happened, she discovered his cock in her mouth too and their movements joined into one rhythm. Soon Estelle heard him cry out and felt him shudder, his prick shooting the most delicious liqueur into her mouth. It was almost like Amaretto, sweet but dusky, and she drank it down greedily, hoping for more. Then Estelle felt her own explosion shaking her to the inner core of her being. More like a volcanic eruption than a mere orgasm, she dissolved into wave upon wave of shivery contractions. Estelle sensed the lava-like flow of her cunt juices as she basked in the glow of glittering lights vibrating all around them. So this was a real afterglow. If it were Eli, Estelle thought, he'd be snoring by now. Instead, she felt herself being kissed all over and each kiss set off another dazzling display of fireworks. She soon realized that she and her lover were the source of these mysterious pulsating lights. Swirling at the center of this tornado, she felt her heart actually melting into his, his into hers, into one heart and she could see his face transforming. For a brief moment, he was her father, then her high school steady boyfriend, then her lifelong idol, Paul Newman, then Josh Shulman, and finally Eli's familiar smiling face appeared. In the next moment, the stranger's face appeared old, almost ancient, and just as quickly he turned into a gurgling newborn baby. Odder still, his face became a mirror image of Estelle herself and he/she looked like a magnificent golden-skinned Goddess. "Yes," she marveled, "it was like a vision of a female God, herself." Estelle thought she heard a voice inside her head murmuring that all of this was nothing special, but was simply a matter of paying attention, something she had never quite mastered in her past life. "Nothing special,

yellow

Estelle," it repeated over and over like a Shamanic chant, as she rested in the ethereal light emanating from and filling her/him with a peace so blissful she could taste it, smell it, embrace it.

Even more outrageous, Estelle could feel that he was still hard. Without any effort, she discovered they were one, his/her penis radiating inside of her/him and the vaginal walls enveloping and joining with the loverod. "This must be paradise, so I guess I didn't wind up in hell after all," Estelle said to herself in a voice giddy with enlightenment.

Below her, Estelle could see Eli talking to her dead body again as the nurses began to wheel her out of the room on a stretcher, but it all seemed rather vague now and almost fuzzy. Out of the corner of her eye, she saw her new lover take some little tool and cut through the silver cord that was still attached to that old lumpy bag of flesh. It didn't even hurt. Nothing hurt anymore. Death was love, formless love. What a hoot!

"I GIVE YOU
    THE LOST

MAP TO
    MY BED"

DAWN SONG: HER

W. A. Fahey

Clear dawn, brand in the sky scouring blueness.
Water fingers playing their routine
On breast, on thigh, one note and another.
Bird song and silence. A pine cone falls.

I want to be taken by God.
I want to be pinned down in a white light and stripped clean.
I want to be stretched like a fall of water.
I want to be entered, entered and filled.

And the cave's echo says "What?" to me.
And the wind with its bracelet of icicles says "What?" to me.
And the sun has already started to wheel up the sky.
And morning is making, making and doing, and it's wet
   on my thigh.

yellow

I GIVE YOU

■

*Anita
Endrezze*

I give you secret horses
wreathed in jasmine.
I give you yellow wine
distilled from aged stars.
I give you my tapering thighs
which are two slender candles
joining in flame.

I give you the power to touch fire.
I give you the dreamy tunnels
midnight makes in our sleep.
I give you my wet hands.

I give you the aquamarine eyes
of rain.
I give you the lost map
to my bed.
I give you my onyx eyes
that see even in the dark
shadows of your thighs.
I give you the noble crown
of love.

I give you the green corridors
grass divides from the wind.
I give you my amber waist
to encircle with the jewels
of your kisses.
I give you this fragrant entrance.
I give you this. I give you this.

I give you the buttons of silence
inside a snail's shell.
I give you the hurricane
of my orgasm.
I give you the evidence of ocean
in my womb.

SILK

■

I give you back the thickened sex
of you: it gives me much pleasure.
I give you back the balance
of your semen: it is full of daughters
with sapphire eyes.
I give you back all that you give me
continuously;
these gifts are ours forever.

yellow

THE ISLAND OF THE MAPMAKER'S WIFE

■

Marilyn Sides

She trades in antique maps. Her small shop is on Congress Street, three blocks from Boston Harbor. Full of history, tourists drop in from Bunker Hill, Beacon Hill and exclaim in surprise, "You're the owner?" They wonder, often aloud, why does this rather young woman, with only a few glinting silver threads in her hair, why does she spend her time behind the tarnished letters *C. M. Descotes* on the dusty window? What makes her hand linger so on the ancient sea-charts as she smoothes out their creases? An unnatural woman, they think, never out loud, to care about latitude and longitude.

The old map-dealers, retired military men and historians in worn tweeds, know better, point out that Descotes is only too predictably a woman. For all her expert abilities—which they admit with grudging respect—to date any map, to attribute it to its designer, to price it for the market, Descotes betrays herself by her specialty. Her passion, the map she knows best and collects for herself, is the frivolous picture map so prized three hundred years ago by fat Dutch wives for their homes.

"Descotes," the dealers reproach her in dismal tones, "merely interior decoration, you know." But it pleases her to think of thin light coming from a window, watery light falling on a white wall spread with a gaily colored map of Europe, Africa—it makes no difference, any annihilation of vast seas and continents to a rectangle will do—bleak light falling further on a table spread with a rich red Turkey carpet, one corner lifted back like a raised skirt. Pure light falling on the woman reading there.

"Ah, Descotes, most unscientific, those maps. Truth? Progress?" But, like her mapmasters, Descotes would sink a newly discovered Alaska for a mermaid billowing her breast on a wave. Descotes would shrink Siberia for a long-whiskered sea monster rolling at the sea-queen's side.

Among the map-dealers, only one indulges her taste without raising an eyebrow. William taught her everything he knew about maps. She learned to love them as much as she loved to pore over his old skin lined and loose until the day, years ago, he decided that he was "Too old for you" and rolled himself up and away from her as she lay still in bed. Between them now there is the cool comfort of shop talk. One afternoon in January, William telephones her from his shop in Salem, a shop with something for people with all sorts of specialities: Indian medicine bags, Chinese chess sets, embroidered chasubles, grass masks with little saucer ears, and maps.

"Two of *your* maps are coming on the market, sweetheart. In Amsterdam, number 4, Prinsengracht. Very fine maps, I hear. Now the dealer's a strange bird, likes to talk out a sale. Won't deal over the telephone. Doesn't care if he loses the business. You're going to have to get up and go there, this time."

"But it's so inconvenient for me to go, right now. I'm expecting offers. You don't have his number, do you? Maybe he'll talk to *me*, I'm good on the phone, you know."

"Sweetheart, not a chance. My friend there says he doesn't even have a number. So, I've said you're on your way and reserved you a seat on the plane for tonight at nine-thirty."

"The maps are good ones, you say, excellent ones? Very good, your friend says? *My* maps, you're sure?"

"Beautiful maps. You won't be disappointed. Good-bye, sweetheart. Good luck."

On a card she writes "Closed 'til Saturday" and tapes it right above her name on the front window. Three days, she tells her answering service. Three days should be enough. No need to loiter once the map is hers. There's nothing else in the world that interests her anymore. For several years, after losing William, before opening her shop, she traveled, cheap drugstore map in hand, to Italy, Mexico, India, anywhere, for months at a time, every chance she had, wide-eyed, ready to snap a picture, ready to exclaim "how strange, how beautiful" to the man next

Yellow

to her whether it was Stephen, Mark, or Bill, willing to stroke the flesh of Stephen, Bill, or Mark lit up by a tropical moon or the northern lights. One morning, however, New Delhi seemed like Paris, like Tokyo, all the same red square on the Michelin maps, the hotels the same black blotches. Bill was as thin, dry, and dark with tiny criss-crossing sentences as Stephen or Mark.

Back in Boston, she "retired," as she likes to put it, and opened her map store. Using her typewriter and her telephone, she manages to find the maps she wants without leaving the city, much less the country. A quiet day spent stroking the downy surface of the thick map paper, then a long walk puffed up and down the shore by fat-cheeked winds, and at last home alone with mad continents of color on the walls—this is a day filled with enough earthly glory for her.

That night the plane cabin seems a prison and a hell. It is drab and smelly, the plastic forks and the passengers make an empty clatter. As the plane rushes past the last lighthouses on the coast and into the blind, shapeless night, she sweats with a fear that, bound to her seat, she can't walk off. She never used to be afraid to fly, what has made her fear to die now? When her mind strays towards the black nothing outside the window—sleep is just as dark, just as much a dense dark fog—she tries to guide it home by sketching out on the airline napkins her favorite maps, so bright, so brimming with ships and flowers and the walls of perfect cities. She makes herself imagine the maps in Amsterdam, very fine maps, William says, very good maps, lovely maps to gaze upon.

In Amsterdam at last, exhausted, she takes a short nap in the hotel room before going to look at the maps. But, she sleeps too long. Waking up in the dark, she angrily reminds herself that there is no time to waste on this trip, and now the shop will be closed. All she can do tonight is walk to the dealer's shop and make sure she knows the way. A good decision, she congratulates herself an hour later, as after several wrong turns in the maze of canals—it has been years since she used a map to find something, the small map is awkward in her hand, the tiny print a strain—she circles towards the shop.

Along Prinsengracht, tall, narrow houses stand stiffly up into the night, the light from their upper rooms blurred by drawn lace curtains in a hundred starry patterns. The maps had better be good, to get her away from home, where she, too, could be behind her curtains in a soft light. Number 4 is a house narrower and darker than all the others. Yet downstairs in the tiny ground-floor chamber there glows a heavily shaded lamp. No one comes, however, when she taps, and taps again louder on the cold glass, a sound too loud in the empty street, a neighbor may look out the window and think she is a thief. The door is locked. Pressed against the window, she makes out the quite good things risked in the window—Renaissance globes, Islamic sextants—the maps will be fine ones. Startling her, a face looms up before her eyes, that of a huge cat, dusky yellow with a white tufted bib, who stretches out between an astrolabe and an ancient tome. The cat shakes his head officiously like an old clerk, as if to say, "Closed. Go away."

A cold winter wind turns through the canals. She has to move on. Walking back down the street, she enters into a pub for some dinner. The customers, mostly men, raise their heads to stare at her, but out of habit she looks only at the waiter, nods to him, and follows him to a small table near the central stove that heats up the dark-panelled room. She orders and soon the food comes, promptly and properly hot. As the waiter sets the plate before her, she thinks how long it took to acquire the ability—self-taught—to enjoy eating alone. To make herself served well and courteously, to eat slowly, enjoying her meal, thinking her own thoughts.

A shout of laughter bursts from a group of men standing behind her in one corner. Startled, she looks over at them and a big, tall man, obviously the teller of the joke, catches her eye with his bright, curious glance. Of course, the laugh was raised

yellow

to make her turn around; it always provokes men, as men, to see a woman alone, making her way without one of them. She must still be quite exhausted to have fallen for that; she knows better. Yet at one time, she suddenly recalls and it's like finding an old dress and thinking instantly of a certain night, at one time, when she used to travel, she would have looked back at this man with a long look and a smile, she would have let him join her for a drink. But now, it's a quiet triumph to have only business on her mind—the maps, her maps, fine maps—once they are in hand she can go home, stay at home. She turns back around, finishes her dinner, pays, and nods good night to the waiter.

In widening circles, squinting at her map over and over, she returns to her hotel and goes to bed. However, having slept too long that afternoon, she sleeps fitfully. Finally falling asleep, she sleeps heavily and wakes up late, again. Rushing through her breakfast, hurrying past canals, she arrives at number 4 by eleven only to find a note saying "Back at eleven-thirty" in Dutch and English. Forced into unwilling tourism, she idles along the canal glancing at the shop windows. But she finds a little pleasure after all. In one window a painting with a map in it, her kind of map, is displayed. A sign she will be successful, she tells herself, and begins to be more cheerful. In the picture only the back of a painter, elegant in a slitted doublet, is visible as he sits before his easel. At the far right corner of the room, placed between a casement window and a heavily carved table, stands a model bedecked with pearls, ostrich plumes, and blue silk brocade. Her face turns slightly away from the artist's gaze. The rival-beauty of the painting is a map of Spain, bordered with panoramic views of the principal cities, which takes up almost all of the back wall. The artist has spent his best efforts on where the light falls from the leaded window—the shirt shining through the doublet on the painter's wide back, the averted cheek of the woman, the gleaming emptiness of sea on the map. These glow in the gloom of the room.

The picture keeps her standing so long enthralled before it that Descotes has attracted the attention of another idler. He has been strolling up and down the street, looking at windows, watching her. She has felt him there, behind her, she realizes. Now he moves closer, in a moment—she remembers how it goes—he will be so close that they will have to say something about the painting, then the weather, then comes an invitation to coffee, to dinner, to bed, if only she keeps standing still for a few more seconds.

But her maps. With a quick glance at her watch she sees it's time for the shop to be open. She turns away as he takes the last step towards her. She used to smile a polite, apologetic smile at moments like these. The practice comes back to her an instant too late now. The man frowns after her.

At number 4, the shop door opens with a grating rumble and shuts with a loud click. The room is as empty as last night, except for the big cat, who rises, stretches, and jumps to her feet. By running at her ankles, he steers her to the desk at the back where the lamp still burns. From the ceiling to the wainscoting are shelves of calf-bound books whose spines glimmer with gold lettering, beneath the shelves wide cabinets of polished drawers, map drawers she knows. A large table blackened with age takes up the rest of the room.

Steps come thumping down some hidden stairs. A big head topped with a shock of red hair ducks through the low door to the left, the heavy body that follows blocks up the doorway. How this body must fill up this thin, narrow house, how it almost looks at this moment that he is some great hermit crab, carrying his fragile shell house on his back.

Then she sees it is the joketeller from the pub. He recognizes her right away, a grin splits his wide round face. She can see how he could make people laugh, to look at him would

yellow

make anyone laugh. His brown corduroy suit hangs flabbily around his thick body. His rumpled white shirt sticks out between the waistband of his pants and the thin belt he has hitched up too high and too tight. Part of his shirttail is even caught in his fly, the tuft of it sticks out like a gay white sail before him. She remembers the quick eyes, she sees they are a rich chestnut, curious and direct. His long thin nose along with these eyes gives him the look of a courtly bird. A very funny man, except, it strikes her sharply, for the lips. They are almost too thin, too severe, the lips of an exacting man. Between the upper part of this face and these lips there must run some invisible fault line, along which the two characters, the clown and the master, strain together unevenly.

She hands him her card. "You were told to expect me, I believe."

Throwing up his hands in exaggerated surprise, he exclaims, "Ah, the map-lover. I should have guessed it was you last night. Loitering around the shop, hoping for even one glimpse, a little lovesick already, no? That's a good sign for the dealer, yes? He can charge what he likes. He knows the customer must have the map."

So she's to be paid back for her coolness in the pub.

"I must say that it is rare to encounter a young woman—oh yes, my dear, to a dilapidated, insomniac, old carcass like myself, I'm broken beyond my forty years—yes, yes, you are young, very young—rare to meet a young someone as fervent as you about their trade. Lingering in the cold night simply to be near the maps." He pauses, notes her annoyance with delight, and then turns mock-professional. "All right, let's be very serious, let's have a look at the maps, the all-important maps."

He bustles over to the locked drawers, at the same time pulling a ring of keys from his pocket. The ring comes out, and along with it an ink pen, a crumpled handkerchief, and a leather change purse that falls to the floor spilling coins all around. "You see how clumsy I am—the customer says to herself, 'The dealer is nervous, the advantage is mine.' " He stops and bends over to pick up the coins. As he stoops over with his back to her, his jacket pulls up, his shirt pulls out of his trousers, and he is exposed almost down to the cleavage of his buttocks. Surprised, she thinks "how ridiculous" and at the same time she wants to place her hand there on that skin, it is so fine-grained, smooth, firm almost luminous as if the whiteness were some sheen of silver melted into gold. She'd like to run her fingers down the ridge of the spine to where it ends, she'd like to feel under her palm the muscles playing there so smoothly and powerfully. This must be the center of power for the big body.

Her body starts to tighten up, her thighs, her belly—it has been a long time since she has longed so sharply to touch someone's flesh, to have the feel of it in her fingertips at that moment, knowing it will linger there like a soothing shock for days. Just as she becomes afraid that her hand will go out of its own accord, he straightens up, the clothes covering him in a clumsy bunching of fabric.

In relief she allows herself to smile, she shouldn't let such a silly thing distract her. The maps are all that counts, the maps and going home. Luckily, he has noticed nothing and, unlocking the drawer, has drawn out a roll and pulled the desk lamp over to the big table. He unfurls the map and with a click turns up the power of the lamp to illuminate a beautiful— William was right—beautiful piece of work.

And with one look at the map she is completely back in her mapworld. Here the Netherlands of 1652 have been painted in as a blue heraldic lion rampant on the northern coast of Europe. She almost laughs, for the lion—in spite of his gold crown and elegant tufted tail—looks like a fat blue cat standing on his hind legs to bat at a fly. He could be the royal cousin of the yellow cat gazing at her from the desk. Turning professional, she admires the coloring, a fine wash of blue bice,

yellow

names the probable date of the map and the map-making firm. Impressed, the dealer cries, "Oh, very good, very good, absolutely right. I shall sigh when you're gone. I see only pretentious amateurs and tourists all day long."

She could maybe afford it at what she estimates its price to be. The map of the Battle of Waterloo that she has been holding onto as the price climbed, she could let that go for this. Finishing the thought, she straightens up. He takes the hint, rolls up the map, and then going back to the drawer he produces the second map.

Before her are every fanciful figure of the East, quaint and funny as in a children's book. Ruling the Mongolian plain, the great Khan twirls his mustaches in front of his golden-tasselled tent. Further south Mandarins bow beside their pagodas. A cannibal couple of Borneo, modest in their grass skirts, look shyly at each other over the human elbows they nibble. In the reaches of the sea, fretted calligraphy, like a handwritten letter home, details the terrible marvels of the world.

As she looks the map over, she almost hums; it's good, it's what she had hoped to see. Her explorer's map of the Belgian Congo, she knows a small, rich museum that covets it. To the dealer, again, she names the date and the mapmaker. He is delighted, of course, she is right. Now to business, she thinks and prepares her offers in her mind.

However, he has one more map to show her. "A special map. It's not for sale, but if you don't mind, I'd like you to see it. It will give me great pleasure to have you appreciate it, oh, not give it a price, simply see how beautiful it is. I'm rather proud of it and like to show off my good taste." While putting back the second map and bringing back the new map, he tells her that the circumstances of the map's purchase were curious. One day, an old woman had summoned him to come look at a map she had for sale. The map was kept in a locked cabinet in her room. Descotes should imagine a big, tall white-haired woman with the smallest of keys on a blue scrap of ribbon, leading him to her bedroom, shutting the door behind them. The map, she told him, was a gift she had made to herself years ago, with some money left to her by her grandmother, a gift she had kept all to herself all these years, until now when she needed the money to, as she laughed, bury herself. When he saw it, he thought how well she had rewarded herself all those years of her life. "Another mapmistress, she was," he grins at Descotes, "though of only this one map." In fact, he felt very humble in front of her, as if she knew the map better than he, an expert, did. After one look at it, he bought it.

Descotes is immediately wary; declaring the map not for sale, telling the odd story of its former owner—he must be setting her up for the map he really wants to sell her today. She prepares herself to give a cold eye to the map.

But when he lays the map before her, she finds it impossible to do anything but gaze upon it with absolute abandonment to pleasure. This map of South America would have seemed to anyone else a very plain map compared with the first two—but she sees right away it is as lavish, even more so in its own way. She has to admit to herself it is the best of the three maps, truly a superb map beyond comparison. The work could only have been done by the best illuminator of maps in the seventeenth century, Margarethe Blau, the wife of the master printer Theodor Blau. The long spine of the Andes, Frau Blau has rendered in the finest golden tincture of myrrh with the western slope reflecting the setting sun in a delicate pink wash of cochineal. Several stands of trees, in a thousand varying shades of green, play the vast rain forest of Brazil. Rivers have been threaded through the continent in indigo banded with magenta. The southern pampas wave their bluish leaves and the golden stalks. Red lead, the color of dried blood, shadows the double cathedral towers of Spanish settlements. Surrounding the land, showing off its gentle brightness, the sea is stippled like shot silk in dark indigo and a wash of lighter blue bice.

yellow

■

As she examines it, what suddenly strikes Descotes about the map is that its very perfection wants to be saying something, like a child perfectly composed at high tension in order to get the attention of its mother. Taking her magnifying glass from her purse, she works down the western coast, around the Horn, and up the eastern coast to the Caribbean. Everything, every inlet and spit of land, every island, is absolutely correct, and Margarethe Blau has blessed her husband's perfect outlines with her rare colors.

No, here is an island, just off the coast of Venezuela, an island out of place, no, not out of place, for it belongs nowhere else. An imaginary island, drawn in with quick strokes of a pen, not printed. This is what the map's perfection silently strains to tell—the error, the gratuitous island.

The dealer sees Descotes staring at the island and laughs in delight. "So, you've discovered the secret of the map. Frau Blau has sketched in her own paradise: 'Let there be an island and an island appeared on the bosom of the sea.' "

The island *is* a lovely Eden, all for oneself. There are minute patches of greenish gold furze, tiny trees toss in a breeze, tender hillocks—and then Descotes gasps, looks again, narrows her eyes. She can hardly believe it, this exquisitely detailed landscape, its contours, take on the breathtakingly precise outline of a woman embracing a man. That faultless drawing of the upper coast, the taut single line is the woman's exposed neck, her back, the curve of her buttocks, the sweep of her legs superbly clean down to the graceful feet tapering off into the ocean. The arched lower coast is the lover's long back, stretched out afloat on the Caribbean waves. He presses up against her breast and belly and thighs, his thighs and legs flail. His arms are outstretched above his head, grasped by her hands. The good Frau must have found it unbearable to show them—her and her lover, some sailor?—crying out in pleasure,

SILK

golden hair falls over the woman's face, the lover's face, it flows into the sea, curling and rushing like foam against the rocky shore.

Staring at the island, Descotes feels her own breasts ache, her face must glisten, again a sharp and sudden excitement makes her almost tremble. It isn't fair to be taken so unexpectedly with longing.

"Quite wonderful, no?"

Of course, he knows! He has set up this scene like a voyeur, forcing this upon her, so he could watch her, shock her. Angry, she cannot look at him, she won't give him the satisfaction.

"You don't find the island delightful? Oh, you must, I would be so disappointed!" He seems genuinely puzzled by her silence, his voice innocent of any smile.

Descotes can hardly believe he cannot see, truly see the island. It is so alive, so terrible a picture of possession. He sees only an island, an idiosyncratic island, not a seizure, a conquest, an establishing of rights. It is as if he were an amateur and hadn't recognized the signature or the distinguishing stamp that would make a valuable map in fact priceless. Would she be dishonest if she doesn't point out the true nature of the island to him? But she cannot bear to, it would be like making him aware of her own body pressing, it seems to, against the very walls of the room. Why should she tell him, if he can't see it himself? "Forgive me. I'm sorry, I was lost in it. It's beautiful." Trying to control the tremor in her voice, she adds, "It's so beautiful I'd like to buy it. Would you sell it to me?"

He laughs in triumph. "I knew you would love it. But, as I said, it's not for sale, I simply wanted you to admire it. Now that your immense expertise has confirmed my judgement, I'm very happy. I shall not regret the enormous sum I paid for it."

Descotes, thinking she hears him working up the price, almost smiles and bites her lips. She sings to herself, he's going to sell, he's going to sell.

yellow

"We all," he continues, "must allow ourselves an extravagance once in awhile, isn't that right? And this is so beautiful." He looks back down at the map with unfeigned pleasure.

"It's a masterpiece, I agree. Name your price."

Surprised by her insistence, he gives her a long look. Then he laughs, "Oh, forgive me, you must think I'm bargaining with you. No, no, I don't make deals that way. With me, business is always very straightforward. I'm sorry, the map is not for sale. I tell you very honestly, I bought it for myself. It called out for someone who would admire it as much as the old woman."

"But it may be that I admire it more than you and as much as she did. Then, by rights, it should be mine."

He stares at her for several moments. Then, as if testing her, he names a price. It is an immense sum. Almost humiliated to show him what the map means to her—but then he doesn't know what she knows—she swallows and says she can raise the sum, if he will sell the map to her.

His silence is rather cruel, since he must know now that he has her, that she would probably give anything to have the map. When he finally speaks, it is in a serious, friendly tone, a tone that strikes her as only too much like that which William uses with her. "I'm older than you, let me protect you from yourself. Take one of the other maps. They are masterpieces, too, albeit gaudy compared to this one. I'll give you a very good deal on them. For this map, I'll make you beggar yourself."

"That's my affair. I know the business as well as you. I still would like to buy the map. All you have to do, it seems to me, is decide to sell it."

He looks down at the map again, stares at it intently, questioning it, searching it for some answer to her. "It is a fine map, very fine, not another like it, so quiet and calm in its mastery, so happy with its lovely island. Is it really worth so much to you? Why, I must ask myself?"

SILK

She manages a crooked smile. "You know women, we have our fancies, our cravings, mine is your map, that's all."

"A woman's weakness? You're that kind of woman, then? Not a map-dealer?" Rolling up the map (oh, my island, gone, she thinks in pain), he puts her off. "Go back to your hotel and think about it. Can you really get the money? I'll see you again at ten o'clock tomorrow. I have to think about it too."

He has to sell to her, he has to give her his word *now*. She wants to argue on, badger him, but she reminds herself, with difficulty, that she has already passed the limit of what is considered civil bargaining among dealers; she consoles herself, with difficulty, that at least she's made him consider selling. Forcing herself to nod, smile, she turns and leaves the shop. Spinning out canal by canal, she hurries back to the hotel and there she places her calls as if she were raising a ransom— quick, a matter of life and death. She lies to the manager of her bank and gets a loan. From William, she demands money. She tells him that it is an invaluable map, that she has to have it. When he argues that it is too expensive for her business, she argues back that if he hadn't taught her to prize maps she wouldn't be in the business at all anyway. For the first time in all these years, she makes him feel he owes her something for making her go away, he has to pay her off with the map. He promises her the money and then with a cool good-bye hangs up.

But she doesn't pause an instant to feel ashamed of herself. Adding up the figures, she finds she has the dealer's price. At first she's elated, in the next second frightened at the thought that she is going to throw all this money away for one map. She hastily promises herself she'll work extra hard this spring, she'll move maps round, she'll deal in ways she's refused to before. She's already thinking how she can strip her favorite maps from her own walls, maps she used to treasure as if they were her children; now, she'll sell them down the river—heartless.

At dinner, she starts to worry again. Is the map worth so much? She sketches and resketches the map on a scrap of

yellow

paper. But her island comes out merely as an island every time. If the island was really that man bound to that woman, he would have seen it. It is only an island, only an island. But, she argues back to her own doubts, the old woman knew it, she kept it secret in her cabinet, an exquisite torment. That was the clue, wasn't it?

She packs, there will not be much time tomorrow to close the deal—he has to sell it!—and make her flight. Trying to sleep, she finds her mind too busy. She is either adding up columns of figures, or sorting out the maps she will have to sell, or attempting to conjure up the island—but it is always only an island. That makes her despair more than she ever has in her life, the very thought of that island being only an island, merely an island.

Only an island—she gets out of bed, gets dressed, she has to go back and look at the island, tonight, she has to know.

Once more, she winds in and in to the shop, by now she has found her footing, she knows every landmark, every bridge, every house along the way. Prinsengracht, number 4, cat, lamplight. The door is open, but at the loud click of its closing no one comes. She goes to the back of the shop and in through the small door. Off to one side is a dark kitchen and on the other nothing but a narrow screw of white stairs. Up and up she goes, up into this whelk. At the top is a large room, most of it in the dark except for a light on the table where he sits in a big chair. His jacket is off, the shirtsleeves rolled up over massive forearms, with gilt hairs glinting. He stares at the map, her map. She walks in and over to the table. Looking down at the map, she sees instantly that she was right, yes, the two bodies taut as one still arch in that sea.

"I have the money. I raised it." She has barely any voice.

His eyes are sharp and black, his lips tightened up, as he looks up into her face as if he would read it. "What do you see in my map?"

Her face is made as smooth, as white as thick paper, her eyes almost closed into thin brushstrokes of black lashes. Provoked by her silence, he pushes his chair back, stands up and steps over to her, watching her closely. "Tell me about my map."

She stays perfectly still and says nothing. If she just waits and stays still he'll have to give her the map, she says to herself over and over, stay still, just wait, let him find his way to giving her the map, it is inevitable that he will give her the map.

"I won't sell it to you."

Oh, mere defiance easily brushed aside, brushed aside with her hands, reaching out, brushing against that big chest, over across the shoulders, down the arms to take the thick forearms in her hands, to steady herself, to grasp the thick forearms, brushed with gold in the light, to steady him, to keep him on course. She holds fast to them, at the wrists, she wants the feel of them in her hands from the very first, she wants to know the sinews, the bone, the muscle, to feel the grace of flesh—her hands had almost forgotten such grace—she wants to promise herself with this grip, to make a claim with this grip, that she will close her lips over his, she will unbutton his shirt and push him back to the bed she sees over his shoulder, there she will free him from that belt, pants, socks and shoes, she will lay him out on that bed, his fine white legs, the knees knotted intricately like silk cording, the thighs, white and firm as ivory, furzed red-gold, she will smooth him out and then raise up with her hand the long thick spit of land from his bristling thicket of gold, raise it up very long and high, then mount it, as the dawn whirls in and in the canals after her, the light falling on her as she mounts him and holds the wrists down, hard, as she leans over to watch his face in exquisite dread, as she pulls herself up on him, then crashes back down, as he cries out sharp and hard against the white walls of that room, as she washes up gasping in the billowed sheets, the cat lolling in the shallows by their side.

yellow

CHINA
SPARKLERS

■

Miriam Dyak

(For Ray)

Your voice cross continent
dream still stuck to my skin in bright day
the road to town takes on sensual dimensions
I want to rub up against cows in pasture
roll with the heifers in shaggy rippled coats
licked smooth by their wide brown tongues

The kind of day in late summer sun
when my skin reddens and I swell like peaches on the tree
such simple things split me open
colors sing out high brass notes to a fast pulse
while the Pointer Sisters throb on the AM
singin' *'bout a man with a slow hand*
'bout a lover with an easy touch . . .

You went like a match to a stick of incense
that set me off on a
long slow sweet burn all day

"THE HOT & WHIRLING

WHITENESS OF
HER ARMS"

THESME
AND THE
GHAYROG
∎

*Robert
Silverberg*

She slept more soundly that night than the one before, although she was still not accustomed to sleeping on the floor in a pile of bubblebush leaves or having someone with her in the hut, and every few hours she awakened. Each time she did, she looked across at the Ghayrog, and saw him each time busy with the entertainment cubes. He took no notice of her. She tried to imagine what it was like to do all of one's sleeping in a single three-month stretch, and to spend the rest of one's time constantly awake; it was, she thought, the most alien thing about him. And to lie there hour after hour, unable to stand, unable to sleep, unable to hide from the discomfort of the injury, making use of whatever diversion was available to consume the time—few torments could be worse. And yet his mood never changed: serene, unruffled, placid, impassive. Were all Ghayrogs like that? Did they never get drunk, lose their tempers, brawl in the streets, bewail their destinies, quarrel with their mates? If Vismaan was a fair sample, they had no human frailties. But, then, she reminded herself, they were not human.

In the morning she gave the Ghayrog a bath, sponging him until his scales glistened, and changed his bedding. After she had fed him she went off for the day, in her usual fashion; but she felt guilty wandering the jungle by herself while he remained marooned in the hut, and wondered if she should have stayed with him, telling him stories or drawing him into a conversation to ease his boredom. But she was aware that if she were constantly at his side they would quickly run out of things to talk about, and very likely get on each other's nerves; and he had dozens of entertainment cubes to help him ward off boredom, anyway. Perhaps he preferred to be alone most of the time. In any case she needed solitude herself, more than ever now that she was sharing her hut with him, and she made a

yellow

long reconnaissance that morning, gathering an assortment of berries and roots for dinner. At midday it rained, and she squatted under a vramma tree whose broad leaves sheltered her nicely. She let her eyes go out of focus and emptied her mind of everything, guilts, doubts, fears, memories, the Ghayrog, her family, her former lovers, her unhappiness, her loneliness. The peace that settled over her lasted well into the afternoon.

She grew used to having Vismaan living with her. He continued to be easy and undemanding, amusing himself with his cubes, showing great patience with his immobility. He rarely asked her questions or initiated any sort of talk, but he was friendly enough when she spoke with him, and told her about his home world—shabby and horribly overpopulated, from the sound of things—and about his life there, his dream of settling on Majipoor, his excitement when he first saw the beauty of his adopted planet. Thesme tried to visualize him showing excitement. His snaky hair jumping around, perhaps, instead of just coiling slowly. Or maybe he registered emotion by changes of body odor.

On the fourth day he left the bed for the first time. With her help he hauled himself upward, balancing on his crutch and his good leg and tentatively touching the other one to the ground. She sensed a sudden sharpness of his aroma—a kind of olfactory wince—and decided that her theory must be right, that Ghayrogs did show emotion that way.

"How does it feel?" she asked. "Tender?"

"It will not bear my weight. But the healing is proceeding well. Another few days and I think I will be able to stand. Come, help me walk a little. My body is rusting from so little activity."

He leaned on her and they went outside, to the pond and back at a slow, wary hobble. He seemed refreshed by the little journey. To her surprise she realized that she was saddened by this first show of progress, because it meant that soon—a week, two weeks?—he would be strong enough to leave, and she did not want him to leave. *She did not want him to leave.* That was so odd a perception that it astonished her. She longed for her old reclusive life, the privilege of sleeping in her own bed and going about her forest pleasures without worrying about whether her guest were being sufficiently well amused, and all of that; in some ways she was finding it more and more irritating to have the Ghayrog around. And yet, and yet, and yet, she felt downcast and disturbed at the thought that he would shortly leave her. How strange, she thought, how peculiar, how very Thesme-like.

Now she took him walking several times a day. He still could not use the broken leg, but he grew more agile without it, and he said that the swelling was abating and the bone appeared to be knitting properly. He began to talk of the farm he would establish, the crops, the ways of clearing the jungle.

One afternoon at the end of the first week Thesme, as she returned from a calimbot-gathering expedition in the meadow where she had first found the Ghayrog, stopped to check her traps. Most were empty or contained the usual small animals; but there was a strange violent thrashing in the underbrush beyond the pond, and when she approached the trap she had placed there she discovered she had caught a bilantoon. It was the biggest creature she had ever snared. Bilantoons were found all over western Zimroel—elegant fast-moving little beasts with sharp hooves, fragile legs, a tiny upturned tufted tail—but the Narabal form was a giant, twice the size of the dainty northern one. It stood as high as a man's waist, and was much prized for its tender and fragrant meat. Thesme's first impulse was to let the pretty thing go: it seemed much too beautiful to kill, and much too big, also. She had taught herself to slaughter little things that she could seize in one hand, but this was another matter entirely, a major animal, intelligent-looking and noble, with a life that it surely valued, hopes and needs and yearnings, a mate probably waiting somewhere nearby. Thesme told

yellow

herself that she was being foolish. Droles and mintuns and sigimoins also very likely were eager to go on living, certainly as eager as this bilantoon was, and she killed them without hesitation. It was a mistake to romanticize animals, she knew—especially when in her more civilized days she had been willing to eat their flesh quite gladly, if slain by other hands. The bilantoon's bereaved mate had not mattered to her then.

As she drew nearer she saw that the bilantoon in its panic had broken one of its delicate legs, and for an instant she thought of splinting it and keeping the creature as a pet. But that was even more absurd. She could not adopt every cripple the jungle brought her. The bilantoon would never calm down long enough for her to examine its leg; and if by some miracle she did manage to repair it, the animal would probably run away the first chance that it got. Taking a deep breath, she came around behind the struggling creature, caught it by its soft muzzle, and snapped its long graceful neck.

The job of butchering it was bloodier and more difficult than Thesme expected. She hacked away grimly for what seemed like hours, until Vismaan called from within the hut to find out what she was doing.

"Getting dinner ready," she answered. "A surprise, a great treat: roast bilantoon!"

She chuckled quietly. She sounded so wifely, she thought, as she crouched here with blood all over her naked body, sawing away at haunches and ribs, while a reptilian alien creature lay in her bed waiting for his dinner.

But eventually the ugly work was done and she had the meat smouldering over a smoky fire, as one was supposed to do, and she cleansed herself in the pond and set about collecting thokkas and boiling some ghumba-root and opening the remaining flasks of her new Narabal wine. Dinner was ready as darkness came, and Thesme felt immense pride in what she had achieved.

She expected Vismaan to gobble it without comment, in his usual phlegmatic way, but no: for the first time she thought she detected a look of animation on his face—a new sparkle in the eyes, maybe, a different pattern of tongue-flicker. She decided she might be getting better at reading his expressions. He gnawed the roast bilantoon enthusiastically, praised its flavor and texture, and asked again and again for more. For each serving she gave him she took one for herself, forcing the meat down until she was glutted and going onward anyway well past satiation, telling herself that whatever was not consumed now would spoil before morning. "The meat goes so well with the thokkas," she said, popping another of the blue-white berries into her mouth.

"Yes. More, please."

He calmly devoured whatever she set before him. Finally she could eat no more, nor could she even watch him. She put what remained within his reach, took a last gulp of the wine, shuddered a little, laughed as a few drops trickled down her chin and over her breasts. She sprawled out on the bubblebush leaves. Her head was spinning. She lay face down, clutching the floor, listening to the sounds of biting and chewing going on and on and on not far away. Then even the Ghayrog was done feasting, and all was still. Thesme waited for sleep, but sleep would not come. She grew dizzier, until she feared being flung in some terrible centrifugal arc through the side of the hut. Her skin was blazing, her nipples felt hard and sore. I have had much too much to drink, she thought, and I have eaten too many thokkas. Seeds and all, the most potent way, a dozen berries at least, their fiery juice now coursing wildly through her brain.

She did not want to sleep alone, huddled this way on the floor.

With exaggerated care Thesme rose to her knees, steadied herself, and crawled slowly toward the bed. She peered at the Ghayrog, but her eyes were blurred and she could make out only a rough outline of him.

yellow

"Are you asleep?" she whispered.

"You know that I would not be sleeping."

"Of course. Of course. Stupid of me."

"Is something wrong, Thesme?"

"Wrong? No, not really. Nothing wrong. Except—it's just that—" She hesitated. "I'm drunk, do you know? Do you understand what being drunk means?"

"Yes."

"I don't like being on the floor. Can I lie beside you?"

"If you wish."

"I have to be very careful. I don't want to bump into your bad leg. Show me which one it is."

"It's almost healed, Thesme. Don't worry. Here: lie down." She felt his hand closing around her wrist and drawing her upward. She let herself float, and drifted easily to his side. She could feel the strange hard shell-like skin of him against her from breast to hip, so cool, so scaly, so smooth. Timidly she rubbed her hand across his body. Like a fine piece of luggage, she thought, digging her fingertips in a little, probing the powerful muscles beneath the rigid surface. His odor changed, becoming spicy, piercing.

"I like the way you smell," she murmured.

She buried her forehead against his chest and held tight to him. She had not been in bed with anyone for months and months, almost a year, and it was good to feel him so close. Even a Ghayrog, she thought. Even a Ghayrog. Just to have the contact, the closeness. It feels so good.

He touched her.

She had not expected that. The entire nature of their relationship was that she cared for him and he passively accepted her services. But suddenly his hand—cool, ridged, scaly, smooth—was passing over her body. Brushing lightly across her breasts, trailing down her belly, pausing at her thighs. What was this? Was Vismaan making *love* to her? She thought of his sexless body, like a machine. He went on stroking her. This is very weird, she thought. Even for Thesme, she told herself, this is an extremely weird thing. He is not human. And I—

And I am very lonely—

And I am very drunk—

"Yes, please," she said softly. "Please."

She hoped only that he would continue stroking her. But then he slipped one arm about her shoulders and lifted her easily, gently, rolling her over on top of him and lowering her, and she felt the unmistakable jutting rigidity of maleness against her thigh. What? Did he carry a concealed penis somewhere beneath his scales, that he let slide out when it was needed for use? And was he going to—

Yes.

He seemed to know what to do. Alien he might be, uncertain at their first meeting even whether she was male or female, and nevertheless he plainly understood the theory of human lovemaking. For an instant, as she felt him entering her, she was engulfed by terror and shock and revulsion, wondering if he would hurt her, if he would be painful to receive, and thinking also that this was grotesque and monstrous, this coupling of human and Ghayrog, something that quite likely had never happened before in the history of the universe. She wanted to pull herself free and run out into the night. But she was too dizzy, too drunk, too confused to move; and then she realized that he was not hurting her at all, that he was sliding in and out like some calm clockwork device, and that waves of pleasure were spreading outward from her loins, making her tremble and sob and gasp and press herself against that smooth leathery carapace of his—

She let it happen, and cried out sharply at the best moment, and afterward lay curled up against his chest, shivering, whimpering a little, gradually growing calm. She was sober now. She knew what she had done, and it amazed her, but more than that it amused her. Take *that*, Narabal! The

yellow

Ghayrog is my lover! And the pleasure had been so intense, so extreme. Had there been any pleasure in it for him? She did not dare ask. How did one tell if a Ghayrog had an orgasm? Did they have them at all? Would the concept mean anything to him? She wondered if he had made love to human women before. She did not dare ask that, either. He had been so capable—not exactly skilled, but definitely very certain about what needed to be done, and he had done it rather more competently than many men she had known, though whether it was because he had had experience with humans or simply because his clear, cool mind could readily calculate the anatomical necessities she did not know, and she doubted that she would ever know.

He said nothing. She clung to him and drifted into the soundest sleep she had had in weeks.

THANK YOU VERY MUCH FOR THE LAST TIME

∎

*Ray Clark
Dickson*

*Finns do not thank each other
for a visit, but wait for
the next meeting.*

Summer days without darkness; winter without light
but for the flare of her body
in firelight; raw/pine rooms, flax/covered chairs,
life brought back
to the 100/year/old bed.
Nakedness steaming in the log/fueled sauna; bodies
color of pink/fleshed salmon trout
found in Baltic inlets; her smell of birch leaves &
juniper berries; her aura, *sisu*,
a pack with pride & the past.
Toasting with frosted glasses of *kokenkorvo*,
a strong schnapps
biting the teeth of laughter with toasts of *Hei &*
Terveydeksi

    to your health

sharing broiled crayfish in dill with barley bread . . .

He felt, in dying, how that cheater War
chose young salmon trout,
caught, sealed, gutted; smoked in the dull drone

yellow

of gunfire
fed with birch branches & bark shavings
in the round old oildrum of the world, lost in deep
pillows
of arctic cloudberries, the hot & whirling whiteness
of her arms . . .

A SHORT HISTORY OF SEX

■

Gary Soto

"Hijo, this is the lightswitch. No pay you bill, no light, and you make babies with no light." This was Grandmother telling me about sex, or hinting about how sex works. If you don't pay up to the PG&E, then all you have to do at night is lay in bed and make love. This was my first introduction to cause and effect, how one thing leads to another. I was eleven, eating a peach from her tree and watching her water the lawn that was so green it was turning blue. Grandma turned the hose on me, said, "Now you play," and squirted me as I ran around the yard with my jaw gripping the peach and my hands covering my eyes.

It was different with my mother, who broke the news about sex while folding clothes in the garage. "You get a girl pregnant, and I'll kill you." No logic there, just a plain simple Soto threat. I felt embarrassed because we had never talked about sex in the family. I didn't know what to do except to stare at the wall and a calendar that was three years old. I left the garage, got on my bike and did wheelies up and down the street, and tried my best to get run over because earlier in the week Sue Zimm and I did things in Mrs. Hancock's shed. It was better, I thought, that I should die on my own than by my mother's hand.

But nothing happened. Sue only got fat from eating and I got skinny from worrying about the Russians invading the United States. I thought very little about girls. I played baseball, looked for work with a rake and poor-boy's grin, and read books about Roman and Greek gods. During the summer when I was thirteen I joined the YMCA, which was a mistake, I thought—grown men swam nude and stood around with hands on their hips. It was an abominable exhibition, and I would have asked for my money back but was too shy to approach the person at the desk. Instead, I gave up swimming and jumped on the trampoline, played bastketball by myself, and joined

Yellow

the "combatives" team, which was really six or seven guys who got together at noon to beat up one another. I was gypped there too. I could have got beaten up for free on my street; instead, I rode my bike three miles to let other people I didn't even know do it to me.

But sex kept coming back in little hints. I saw my mother's bra on the bedpost. I heard watery sounds come from the bathroom, and it wasn't water draining from the tub. At lunch time at school I heard someone say, "It feels like the inside of your mouth." What feels like that? I wanted to ask, but instead ate my sandwich, drank my milk, kicked the soccer ball against the backstop, and then went to history, where I studied maps, noting that Russia was really closer than anyone ever suspected. It was there, just next to Alaska, and if we weren't careful they could cross over to America. It would be easy for them to disguise themselves as Eskimos and no one know the difference, right?

In high school I didn't date. I wrestled for the school, the Roosevelt Rough Riders, which was just young guys humping one another on mats. I read books, ate the same lunch a hundred times, and watched Mrs. Tuttle's inner thighs and thought, "It's like the inside of your mouth," I watched her mouth; her back teeth were blue with shadows, and her tongue was like any other tongue, sort of pink. I wanted a girl very badly and went around with my shirttail pulled out, and once almost had a girlfriend except she moved away, leaving me to walk around eating a spam sandwich.

My mother's bra on the bedpost, my sister now with breasts that I could almost see behind her flannel nightgown. One night my brother bragged that he knew for sure it felt like a mouth and in fact was drippy like half-chewed peaches. In the dark I scrunched up my face as I imagined baby peaches falling from a dark hole.

I had to have a girl. I was desperate. I stuffed Kleenex in my pants pocket and went around with no shirt. I thought of

Sue Zimm. But she was now lifting weights and looking more like a guy than a girl, which confused me even more, especially when George from George's Barber rubbed my neck and asked me how it felt. I told him it felt OK. He asked if I was going steady, and I told him that I sort of was, except my girl had moved away. He said that it was better that way because sometimes they carried disease you couldn't see for a long time until it was too late. This scared me. I recalled touching Sue when I was thirteen and wasn't it true that she coughed a lot. Maybe something rubbed off onto me. I bit a fingernail, and walked home very slowly. Years passed without my ever touching a girl.

I was twenty, the only guy who went around eating spam sandwiches in college, when I had my first girlfriend who didn't move away. I was a virgin with the girl whom I would marry. In bed I entered her with a sigh, rejoiced "Holy, holy" to my guardian angel, and entered her again. I couldn't believe what it looked like. While my girl slept I lowered myself on an elbow and studied this peach mouth, squeeze thing, little hill with no Christian flag. Pussy was what they called it: a cat that meowed and carried on when you played with it very lightly.

"AH, PEACE
TO YOU, SISTERS

AND BROTHERS,
PEACE TO YOU ALL!"

MAGIC

∎

*Steven
DaGama*

Were I a magician whose wand
taps Shetland ponies into tiger cubs,
I could will myself behind you
and with white-gloved fingers release
the doves of your breasts, and
stroke them and stroke them until macaws
looped the loop from our mouths.

WINTER
RIDDLE

∎

*Steven
DaGama*

A raga needled the ribs
of winter. You unlaced the bodice

of your popular summer dress,
bunched the skirt around

the shirred waist, and draped
your thighs over the arms

of a wing chair. You tasted like
cinnamon and pomegranate.

yellow

CYNTHIA

■

*Susan
St. Aubin*

Anne climbed the back steps to Richard's apartment one Friday evening and peered through the window in the kitchen door before knocking. This time Richard wasn't waiting for her alone, running his left hand through his short gray curls as he read papers from his literature classes, he was drinking coffee with a tall, slender woman dressed in a gray skirt and white silk blouse tight over her small round breasts, her dark hair tied off her face with a piece of black velvet ribbon. She was perhaps in her mid-forties, but it was hard to tell: when she threw her head back and laughed, she was like a girl of sixteen, and when she looked down at her veined hand on the table and frowned, she was like a woman of fifty. She got up and went to the sink with her coffee cup, moving like a dancer, her clinging flannel skirt showing the ripple of her muscles.

Anne remembered then that she'd seen her in front of Richard's apartment building the first time she'd gone there six months ago. The woman had been waiting for a cab, which pulled up as Anne rang Richard's doorbell; she'd thought nothing of it at the time, though the woman had stared at her with penetrating black eyes as if she knew Anne, just twenty years old, wearing jeans and a tight blue tee-shirt, was on her way to her first affair with a professor.

It began to rain lightly. Richard looked up to check the clock on the wall above the door, saw her, and jumped to his feet. "Anne, come in! You're early." He opened the door with one hand while the other played with his hair. The woman turned around and leaned against the sink, smiling.

"Not so very early," said Anne. "It's almost five."

"Anne, this is Cynthia."

Cynthia held out her hand. "I was just leaving. How nice to meet you at last. I've heard so much about you."

Anne was startled by the coldness of her fingers; her smile, too, seemed cold. Richard went with Cynthia to the front door.

When he came back, Anne was sitting at the kitchen table staring at her brown boots. He lifted her long blond hair off her neck and pulled it gently over one shoulder, stroking it like the pelt of an animal. "Why don't you take off your coat? Cynthia's a very old friend. I wish you wouldn't come creeping up the back stairs like that, you might see all sorts of things you'd rather not."

Anne stood up to take off her coat. Richard ran his hand over her breasts, then kissed her, sliding his tongue between her lips and teeth, which she opened somewhat reluctantly, still brooding about Cynthia. She knew she wasn't the only student he invited to his flat; their Friday nights were just one night out of seven, and they occasionally exchanged smiles when they passed in the school corridors. She allowed him to lead her to the bedroom.

"You're still upset, aren't you?" He unbuttoned her dress, let it slide to the floor, pulled her slip over her head, pulled her tights down over her hips, and knelt before her to kiss her mons. She held her legs together, but felt herself loosen as his tongue worked its way between the folds.

He undressed, and they lay on the waterbed in the middle of the room while he stroked her breasts with one hand and her cunt with the other, fingers dipping into her wetness, until she came with a shudder, one hand stroking and clutching his penis. Then he slid his penis inside her and she gripped it with her vaginal muscles, gripping and relaxing rhythmically until he came; and the force of his coming so excited her that she came again, unexpectedly, gasping, then laughing.

"Why did you laugh?" He seemed disturbed.

"When I get something I don't quite expect, I sometimes do." She looked up at the Indian print cloth with tiny mirrors woven into the fabric which he had tacked to the ceiling above the bed like a canopy, while he slowly stroked her breasts and belly. After a while they got under the covers and slept.

In the night she felt him kissing and rubbing against her;

she felt his penis grow hard against her buttocks as he stroked her breasts from behind. She reached back and guided him into her cunt. He kissed her lips and stroked her face and breasts. But how could that kiss be his if he were behind her? There were two hands on her breasts, different hands, one slimmer and smoother than the other; the hands stroked and clasped one another as much as they stroked her. She felt smooth straight hair brush across her face and breasts. Then she came with more intensity than she had ever known, and was unconscious.

Later she woke briefly and felt herself between two bodies. She assumed that she was still dreaming, that the other incident had been a dream, and that this was a continuation of that dream. She slipped into dreamlessness.

In the morning she woke alone in Richard's big bed with sunlight pouring in the window: they'd forgotten to close the curtains. She could hear his coffee grinder whirring in the kitchen, water running, and the clatter of cups. When she shut her eyes, she noticed a scent that was neither hers nor Richard's, a sweet musk that seemed to permeate the sheets. She remembered her dream, that sense of another body, a woman's body, in bed with them.

Richard brought her a cup of coffee, and carefully sat on the edge of the bed with his mug.

"I had a dream," she said.

"Oh?" He seemed to have anticipated this conversation.

"I dreamed there was a third person in bed with us, a woman, I think, but I'm not sure. I was making love with you, and then there was this other person kissing me, and you, and stroking both of us."

He smiled. "Sounds like something you'd like to do, maybe. Dreams are just fantasies of all the things we don't allow ourselves to do in real life."

"No, I don't think so—it's something I've never thought of." She watched the steam rise from her coffee cup.

SILK

"The dream means you must have, at some level. Dreams don't lie."

She was still troubled. "The funny thing is, it didn't feel like a dream."

He snorted. "What do you mean, feel like?"

"My dreams usually feel like dreams. I always know when I've been dreaming. But this—I know it must have been a dream, it couldn't have happened, but it didn't feel like a dream. It was real."

He laughed. "Come on, it was a dream. I've had dreams like that before, everyone has. The dream you think must have been real is probably the dream you most want to be real."

"I've never had a dream like this."

"Then it's your first. I've been present for lots of your firsts, haven't I?" He put her coffee cup gently on the floor beside his before getting into bed with her. "I'll have to find us another woman just to keep you happy."

"You're putting dreams in my head, that's what it is! *You* want another woman with us." Though she laughed into his armpit, she half believed what she was saying.

"Is it something you might want to try?"

She shook her head. "No."

"Think about it."

She shook her head again.

But she did think about it after she left his house at noon; she thought about it for the rest of the week. Before her biology class she asked Nina, who was five years older and claimed to be bisexual, if she'd ever made love with a man and a woman together. Nina dropped her pen and bent under the desk to get it. Sitting up red and flushed, she said, "No, I never wanted to; sex is too personal a thing for me. I've been asked, but no orgies." She spoke very fast; other students were coming into the lecture hall.

Later, Nina asked her if this was something Richard

Yellow

wanted to do. Nina was the one person Anne had told about Richard, and she seemed to disapprove of the relationship, though Anne couldn't think why. Now she said to Anne, "Don't let yourself be pushed into something you can't handle. Be sure you know what you want, that's all. Don't let Richard talk you into it."

Anne nodded. "I won't. But it's something I've been thinking of, too; it's not just an idea he put in my head." She thought of her dream, the dream she almost suspected Richard of planting in her mind, if such a thing were possible. But even if he had, he had created a desire within her which she now felt was her own. "He did suggest it," she admitted to Nina, "but only because I had a dream about it."

Nina lifted her eyebrows. "Oh? Well, in that case . . ." She laughed. "I definitely think you should pay attention to dreams."

"Or pay attention to what you want to do," said Anne. "Even if someone else suggested it first."

It was windy on the lawn where they sat. Anne's hair blew up behind her head like a huge yellow fan, and Nina's short bronze curls twisted and turned. Anne was thinking of Cynthia; she was certain Cynthia was the woman she had dreamed about.

"There is one woman I'd like to make love to, with you," she told Richard that Friday. "Cynthia."

He ran his left hand through his hair and smiled. "I'd like to invite you to dinner together. I'm sure she'd enjoy talking to you. But you can't push anything. If we feel like going to bed together, that's fine, and if not . . ." He trailed off. They made a date for two weeks from Saturday.

"Is Saturday her night?" Anne asked.

Richard laughed. "I'm not quite that obsessive."

Anne dreamed of Cynthia for the next two weeks. On the Saturday of their dinner date, Anne bathed and dressed with extra care, putting on a long beige dress of a nylon fabric that clung to her breasts and body. Over the dress she wore a mohair scarf of a lighter beige and a long trench coat. She looked at her reflection in the mirror on the door to her room as she left, and added a mohair hat that matched the scarf.

When she got to Richard's, Cynthia was already there, very elegant in a brown and beige striped skirt and bronze blouse, her straight brown hair falling loose on her shoulders. She was slicing tomatoes for a salad at the kitchen counter. Richard wore his jeans, as he always did on weekends. Anne sniffed the familiar aroma of Richard's specialty, chicken stuffed with cashews and French bread crumbs. Cynthia greeted her with a smile, as though she already knew Anne quite well, though Anne had only met her once, and took Anne's hand in both of hers.

"I've brought some strawberries," she said. "Do you want to help clean them?"

Anne was glad to have the strawberries to wash. She carefully cut the stem from each one, then sliced them and covered them with brandy and a little sugar.

"A dessert salad," she said to Cynthia.

Richard had set the table, and sat in the middle with Anne and Cynthia at either end.

"Wonderful chicken," said Cynthia. "I'd forgotten how wonderful."

Richard smiled at her. "More stuffing?" he asked Anne.

"The stuffing's Richard's invention," Cynthia explained to Anne. "I love French bread, so we always had leftover stale ends of it in the house."

There was an uncomfortable silence as Anne realized they must have lived together. For a moment, she felt like an intruder in their home.

"Now I just buy a loaf and use it fresh," said Richard.

Cynthia laughed. "Yes, and it tastes so much better this way." She got up, cleared their plates, and brought the bowl of

Yellow

strawberries to the table. "Would you like to dish them up?" she asked Anne, and Richard put three small cut-glass dishes beside the bowl.

Anne spooned the strawberries and syrup into a bowl for Cynthia, then Richard, before serving herself. After they finished eating, Richard lit a cigarette while Cynthia cleared the table and poured them each a cup of coffee, which they sipped in silence. When Anne looked anxiously at Richard, he smiled at her. Cynthia looked from one to the other and laughed.

"Why are we being so silly?" she asked. She put her hand on Anne's. "Richard has told me everything about you, but I see he's told you nothing of me, which may be just as well."

Richard looked out the window.

Anne looked at Richard, then Cynthia.

"Have you ever made love to a woman?" asked Cynthia.

"No," Anne answered.

"Never?" Cynthia smiled and raised her eyebrows.

They sat silently around the table a bit longer, Richard still looking out the window, Cynthia looking at Anne, and Anne looking down at her hands folded around her coffee cup, listening to her own breathing, which seemed like the loudest sound in the room. Richard got up and went into the bedroom; after a bit, Anne and Cynthia followed. While Richard lay nude on the bed, watching and smoking a cigarette, Anne and Cynthia undressed in a quick, business-like fashion, like going to the doctor, Anne thought. She watched Cynthia take off her skirt, her silk blouse, her half slip.

Richard stood up to stroke Cynthia's shoulders, then unhooked her brassiere from behind. Anne thought she had a very nice body, smooth skinned, slender, still lightly tanned from the summer. She saw one small white breast released from its lace cup, and then, where the other should be, a white scar across her chest. Anne felt her breath stop, then catch, then start. Of course mastectomies were common; her own mother had had one, yet she had never seen the scar. It wasn't nearly

SILK

as bad as she had imagined: some horrible disfiguration, the breast chopped away, leaving a gaping hole or a circle of red scar tissue like a burn. Cynthia's neat white scar, leaving no trace of breast, barely noticeable beneath her brassiere, was something Anne hadn't been prepared for. She gently touched the breast, caressing the nipple, which hardened under her palm.

"You see," said Cynthia, "I still have one."

Anne's fingers traced the scar.

"Yes, I had cancer, of course. The usual reason. They told me I had no choice. I think they were right; as it was I . . ." Here she stopped as though there were something she could not admit just yet. To Anne she looked very healthy, but perhaps she was not expected to live.

Anne kissed the scar. "Does it hurt?"

"No, not now."

Anne fastened her mouth to the nipple and circled it with her tongue, sucking lightly and thinking of her mother, who had never revealed her scar. Cynthia stroked Anne's hair. It seemed to Anne that Richard had disappeared; she wanted no one but Cynthia. Then she felt him behind her, his swollen penis poking the small of her back as he reached around to her breasts.

The three of them moved to the bed, where Anne lay back while Richard and Cynthia stroked her full breasts. It was like being an infant, she thought, cared for by a mother and father, but what parents these were! While Richard massaged and licked her breasts, Cynthia ran her tongue down Anne's belly, moving it rapidly in and out of her navel, continuing down to her mons, blowing gently in the light brown pubic hair while sliding her tongue around the clitoris.

Anne heard herself moan. Never had she felt such a certain knowledge of her body and its response from a lover. As Cynthia flicked her tongue over the tip of Anne's clitoris, they both began to breathe faster. Richard sat by Anne's head strok-

Yellow

ing her hair and her breasts while she moaned and twisted and then called out, feeling as though she had been struck by a flash of lightning that went all the way through her and out her toes.

She panted and swallowed; her throat was very dry. Cynthia lay on top of her, her breast soft and the other half of her flat and hard as a man. Anne stroked her shoulders. They rolled over and lay on their sides, still stroking, until slowly Anne slid one hand between Cynthia's legs.

She had never touched another woman like this before. It was so much like touching herself, but with no sensation, that she was frightened. She felt as if she were numb; she could feel nothing but a moist softness on her fingers, like the inside of a sun-ripened peach or plum. It must be like this, she thought, to know braille, to read a book with your fingers. She had to learn through her fingers what pleased Cynthia. Tracing over the hood of the clitoris, she heard Cynthia moan. The right side moved her more than the left; a finger sliding around the opening to the vagina was as pleasurable for her as it was for Anne. Slowly she tested the area, remembering what she liked; and what she liked, Cynthia seemed to like. The soft sensation of ripe fruit was becoming a part of her: when she touched Cynthia, she could feel herself grow swollen and wet, and moved her fingers, still wet from Cynthia's cunt, to her own while she bent her mouth to Cynthia's clit and, as Cynthia had to hers, flicked it with her tongue.

The taste was the same taste of a man, only more intense, more salty and fish-like, with a sweetness quite unlike the bitterness of sperm. Hesitant at first, Anne stuck her tongue deeper into the folds, and finally thrust it into the vagina, testing, tasting. Richard lay on the other side of Cynthia, and while Anne was tasting the new soft fruit, she stroked Richard's hard penis. She moved her lips back to Cynthia's clit again, while with one hand she guided Richard's penis from behind into Cynthia's cunt. Anne kept her thumb and forefinger circled firmly around the base of his thrusting penis while she continued to stroke Cynthia's clit with her tongue.

Cynthia moaned, then screamed: Anne followed her as she thrashed about, never stopping even when she came, but going on while she climaxed again and again, stronger each time, until she was very still, gasping for breath. Richard withdrew then, and Anne took his penis in her mouth while Cynthia's fingers stroked her clit. Richard's penis still tasted of Cynthia; when he came she sucked and swallowed his sperm, which seemed to have a little of Cynthia's sweetness mixed with his bitterness. They fell asleep all three together, Anne in the middle. When Anne woke at dawn, Cynthia was gone, as though she'd been a dream. She snuggled closer to Richard and slept again.

In the morning she asked Richard why Cynthia had left.

"I don't think she'll be back," he told her. "I think she's done what she wanted to." He refused to say more, so she didn't push him.

On her own she looked for Cynthia—on campus, in stores, on the street. She realized she knew nothing about her; she didn't know where she worked, what she did, or where she lived. Once in a downtown department store she thought she saw her standing erect in a rust-colored, clinging dress, talking to the woman behind the jewelry counter, but when she turned around, it wasn't Cynthia.

Without Cynthia, Anne found the relationship with Richard uninteresting. Gradually they saw less of one another; she heard he had a new young girlfriend and didn't care, except when she thought the two of them might make love with Cynthia. Richard was her link to Cynthia; she realized she would most likely never meet Cynthia again except through him. She asked him about her the last Friday they were together.

"I haven't heard from her," he said sharply, but with sadness. "I think she's gone away."

"Where?"

yellow

"I don't know." He shrugged. "She didn't say."

"Away from the city?"

"Oh, yes. She's not here anymore."

"But didn't she tell you where?"

"No." He got up to carry their cups to the sink. Anne knew their relationship had nothing more for her, and mourned the loss of Cynthia more than the loss of Richard.

She grew friendlier with Nina. When spring semester started, they had lunch together on the lawn almost every day. Anne never spoke of Richard, but one day Nina asked if she still saw him.

"No," said Anne. She looked up at two seagulls circling in the clear sky just above them. "I think I'm in love with a woman friend of his."

Nina lay on the grass, her chin cupped in the palms of her hands. "Oh, yeah?"

"But I haven't seen her in months." Anne wasn't sure if she should tell Nina about the night she'd spent with Richard and Cynthia, but decided to go ahead. At the first mention of Cynthia, Nina sat straight up.

"He knows another woman named Cynthia?" she asked.

"I only know this one, I didn't know there was another." And Anne went on with her story, putting in details of their lovemaking she thought would be particularly exciting to Nina. She even told of Cynthia's scar, and of her feeling of fear at first, then acceptance, even an erotic acceptance, of Cynthia's deformity.

"But that's extraordinary," said Nina. "That can't be! You see, I knew Richard's wife. Her name was Cynthia. She died about seven years ago, of breast cancer."

Anne felt her heart jump. "He never told me he'd been married, he never said anything about a wife."

"But the woman you described, that's Cynthia, his wife. If it weren't impossible, I'd say it was her. How amazing, he's actually gone and found somebody just like her." Nina pulled blades of grass from the lawn and piled them beside her knee. "He probably called her Cynthia because she looked like his wife. Maybe he even made her have a breast amputated so she'd be Cynthia all over again. No, that's ridiculous. The whole thing is ridiculous." She continued to pick at the grass, looking down at her hand. "You see, Cynthia, his wife, was my first lover. I was fifteen. She was my ballet teacher. She'd been a dancer with the San Francisco Ballet, a very minor dancer, but to me she was wonderful; I'd never met anyone like her before. And Richard was—well, in the way. I never liked him, I could never understand why she didn't just leave him. But she loved him." Nina looked at Anne. "They were in love. There's not many couples you can say that about, and have it mean anything. And then, after I'd known her a few months, she had her surgery and my parents sent me away to school in Vermont— they figured out what was going on and couldn't get me off the West Coast fast enough. Three years later when I came back, she was dead. And Richard was playing around with students, but not me. He really wanted me, of course, in memory of Cynthia I guess. But no way, I could never stand him."

While Nina talked, Anne remembered the texture of Cynthia's skin, the feel of her hair as it brushed across her arm. It was as if Cynthia were there with them on the lawn. Anne felt her hands tighten into fists. "Do you believe in ghosts?" she asked Nina. "Do you think such a thing is possible, I mean Cynthia coming back to make love with us?"

"No, I don't. Though it's just the kind of thing she would do." Nina smiled. "No, I don't believe it, but I do believe Richard is looking for his wife, and found a woman just like her, and called her Cynthia. That's what I believe."

Anne lay on her back and looked at the sky. The seagulls were gone. When she shut her eyes she felt something like silk brush her leg, and smelled Cynthia's perfume. She opened her

yellow

eyes. Nina was a few feet away, staring into the grass, her eyebrows pressed together.

Anne felt the ghost of Cynthia rise from her mind and disappear like a mist. Real or not, she was gone now. Nina's hair was golden red in the sun. Anne could almost feel the heat of its color. She rolled closer.

SUNDAY MORNING

■

*Steven
DaGama*

Earlier, the sycamore shed tablets of bark;
our concupiscent snow lovers thawed
into a tentative Henry Moore. No tanks,
no husks of automobiles in the yard,
nor blistered orphans braining a rat
with gearshifts. I was listening
to Rostropovich perform slit-eyed,
in ecstasy, Schumann's *Concerto
for Cello and Orchestra in A minor*.
I did not hear you enter the room.
At a folding picnic table jammed between
footboard and wardrobe, I had solved
a poem. Oh yes, a serious poem, yes.
Upon its publication six ambassadors
will escort us to Geneva. I did not hear
you, darling, I heard *tink-tink-tink*
—the saucer, spoon and teacup
you set aside. I did not see you until
I saw you foreshortened as now,
stretching, stretching among the drifts
of our white comforter, conducting
the Leningrad Philharmonic Orchestra.
Your sheer high arches caress
the footboard posts, a silken light
glimmers at the end of the tunnel
of your skirt . . . I strum down the snagged
Venetian blind, spot a martin pecking
a sycamore tablet—blowzy bird-poet,
darling. You are the cynosure
of this morning's arts. My tablet
flittered shut: *Ah, peace to you,
sisters and brothers, peace to you all!*

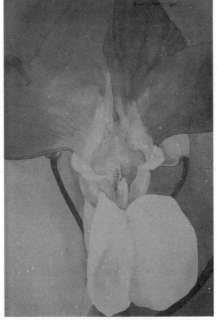

"MOTHER
THE FLESH

FORGIVES
EVERYTHING"

**MOTHER
THE FLESH**

■

*Wanda
Coleman*

has no logic
knows no reason
its tongue his tongue my tongue
tongues. nations

    he is peach
    and i am hot cocoa red

ocean our sweat swells threatens this small island/bed
danger of drowning so real

mother flesh

knows no season. springs forth age after ice age
defies time form climate. is isomorphic
cycles of being felt in the cellular rhythm & blues of essential

        blood vs. stone

spins shakes trembles tremors rots rejoices burns boils fails feels
corrupts conquers hurts hungers maddens moves
withers wonders pains pleases asks answers
dares damns dreams

dear mama the flesh

i know. knowing does not control. you know. how long w/papa?
w/poverty? raising us almost alone
nights crying while we clung to the TV. those creditors
taking your blood for his. the other partners. the late hours
the sweatshop cold settling into your shoulders
the vacant aspirations. then know me

  he is sea fresh sand
  i am fine shellacked cedar

       blood on stone

mama the meat

yellow

is why. is sustenance. strengthens. makes best nada
hip to hip. sperm & egg. muscle music. sweet sweet sweet
tastes like roses smell. goes down gentle. satisfies head, heart,
hope and the god's eye. sanctifies

(sucka fo' love sucka fo' love sucka fo' love)

    he is apricot silk
    i am cinnamon tea

ma flesh is

the battle ground on which truth is ever victor
death a smile and wealth the welcoming arms of children

                    bloodstone

now i enter the temple. such walls. they tower
humbled i feel yet a speck yet a consciousness consuming ALL
kneel

he is with me
yet away from me
in me
yet outside of me
one

it's good. it's good. it's good.

mother
the flesh forgives everything

SON DAYS

∎

Roberta Swann

My big wax belly is eight months gone. These past few months, Jake is feeling neglected. One need only contemplate his remarks.

"You're neglecting me."

He looks at my plethoric state and sneers.

"I thought babies came from cabbages."

How do you explain to your six-year-old son that you can breathe while walking? He's a curious mixture of his naturalist father and me, his undefinable mother.

"How'd you like to take a trip to the country—just you and me, boy?"

His eyes widen and he breaks out into a grin, his tiny teeth tight as corn kernels. We drive to our summer house. Or winter house, depending on the season. In either case, a magic house. Magic, because there's always a row of something ripening on the kitchen sill. Walking up the driveway, he offers me some dusty raisins from his pocket. Chewing, I pat the pea-green Chrysler that hasn't run since 1961 and sits like a sculpture in the garden. He rummages deep into another pocket and comes up with a cookie.

"Want half?"

"No thanks, Jake, you eat it. You're becoming a real string saver like your dad."

We settle on the old sofa, sipping hot chocolate. He stares at my belly.

"Ugh. It's wiggling."

I pull him closer to feel the baby, hoping for a tender moment. He belts me in the gut.

"Why did you do that? It hurts."

"It started first."

Not to dwell on impossible things, we take a walk. The country is fine this time of year. Gazing up at the evergreens pluming the sky, my mood melts and shifts. Walking further

Yellow

into woods, we leave fresh tracks in crusty snow. Jake jolts to a stop.

"Ssshh."

We catch a flash. A doe leaps across the snow drifts. She has a white patch on her buttock and runs with a lifted tail.

"Nature is a relief from people," Jake says after a while.

"Wish you'd parrot my bumper stickers too, Jake, my boy."

We head back in silence. I love this place. Jake does too. All else loses import when we're here together. I trip over the rain-gauge.

"Dad will be mad as hell."

"We'll fill it with three inches of tap water—that's about average for this time of year."

He nods. There's an old washtub rusting near the shed.

"Can I have a bath in that thing?"

"Sure, why not?"

But it's no easy task carrying it inside, cleaning it up, pumping water from the clover-edged well and heating the water on a double burner. I work cheerfully. An hour later I scoop in some Ivory Snow for bubbles.

"All set," I yell.

"Changed my mind."

"Listen, kid, don't mess with me—I'm bigger and stronger than you. And this was your idea, so hop in."

It's a chase around the room. I tackle and pin him to the floor, flinging socks and shirt, carrying him wriggling under-arm, and dump him in the tub. Happy with the game, he sits submerged except for his head and knees sticking out. I throw in the equivalent of a rubber duck. Smacking his bottom, which fits into my hand like a kitchen sponge, there's a loud gurgling sound. A bubble rises. I perch my finger to catch the circle of air.

"You're cute, Mom."

■

I start to scrub his small body. Polish his face, soap his cordy arms and delicate wrists. His lips purse into a bee-sting and he kisses my neck as I stretch in search of the slippery bar of soap.

"You're a sexy little devil."

"Angel."

I scrub his skin as sanguine as our moment.

"You're lucky to have your own personal slave."

"Lucky, schmucky."

I pinch his arm and fall back on the floor pretending exhaustion.

"Didn't you forget something?"

Jake points down to his penis. My hand submerges with the imperious demands of childhood and I rub him with a washcloth. His body relaxes against me. For the first time all day he seems completely tranquil. Self-conscious, I stop. He catches my arm.

"Don't stop. It's really dirty."

Wino, the neighbor's liver-spotted dog, wanders in and starts lapping the water. I swat him with a wet cloth and he sulks out. Wiping his noseprints off my sleeve, I lift Jake from the tub, giftwrapping soft skin in a terry towel. If there's one reward in motherhood, it's this.

Carrying him into the bedroom, I plunk him down. I hand him pajamas.

"It's only five o'clock," he squawks.

"So whadda ya want, your evening clothes?"

Peeling down to bare skin, I discard my damp jeans. He stares at my swollen body.

"You look bigger and stronger this way, but I like you better when you wear shorts—like last summer when those men whistled."

yellow

He unwraps a piece of bubble gum that's been sitting on the dresser. I get into my great woolen robe with the silk tassel, an heirloom from my dead father. Just about to sash it, Jake takes the pink wad out of his mouth and stuffs it into my bellybutton.

"Now the dumb kid can't come out."

We prepare dinner. Jake takes out spoons and saucepans. I peel potatoes. He shells peas. The kitchen window looks out on the woods. We follow the wind shaking a beard of snow off the maple. After dinner, we play games and cards and name the animals we see flickering in the fireplace. The wind picks up and slaps the doors and windows. We sleep double in one bed under a patchwork of quilts. He pushes my hand between his legs and I listen to soft breathing. Though people seldom love one another forever and exclusively, sometimes they do.

SILK

MOTHER & CHILD

■

*Roberta
Swann*

She spent the day feeling frustrated, sipping with ladies who shape their lives around teacups. One hand held a cigarette. The other played with crumbs on the table. She switched from first to third person and managed to be amiable. When they were gone, she invented her life as it went along.

Jennifer walked in, fresh mud on her knees, ready for a bath. Daughter, so blonde and blue, who saw only a little, but with great intensity. She turned on the bathwater and added Jennifer's favorite scent. The child climbed in with a wooden spoon, a rubber frog and a toothpaste cap. The bath, her plaything, she stayed in long enough to shrivel into a white raisin.

She walked into the bedroom and took off her clothes. Body looked thin, but breasts and ass were firm. He said she looked haggard the last time he picked the child up, but ex-husbands are not reliable sources. She slipped into a kimono and propped herself on a pillow. From inside the bed table, she retrieved a vibrator. Muffling the buzz with her discarded panties, she aimed for target. She began to feel feral, as if her clitoris were a magnetic needle gone wild. And then she felt relief. And then she felt sexier.

Lost in her own fantasies, she didn't notice the child trail in until she felt a damp hand ask a question. Flicking off the switch nervously, she got busy with a towel. Never had a child been so meticulously rubbed and powdered. And kissed—to keep that little mouth closed.

"What were you doing?"

"Oh, just giving myself a massage."

"Can I have one too?"

"No, sillyhead, little girls don't get massages."

"Why not?"

yellow

"They don't need them."

"Doesn't it feel good?"

"Yes, Jen, it feels very good. Relaxing . . . "

"So, I want to feel good too."

The child touched her mother's arm, waiting.

"O.K. Lie down."

Jennifer cast off the bathtowel and dug a comfortable place for herself in the bedcovers. The machine skimmed her small body and flushed Jennifer's creamy skin.

"It makes me feel ticklish."

The mother smiled and encouraged intimacy. Jenny stared at her mother's breast that had slipped out of the robe and hung free. The child reached up and squeezed the nipple.

"Look, it changed into magic dots."

Jenny fiddled with her tiny nipplets, then pulled a face.

"Nothing happened."

The mother smiled. What else could she do?

"Buzz my cunny."

She scooped the child in an affectionate hug, cradling her head, rocking.

"Buzz me. Buzz me like you did to your cunny."

Seized by the moment, she loomed down at her creation, a miniature of herself with just the right amount of fingers and toes. A Fabergé egg of a body, the mother thought. Not an immaculate conception this, but miraculous. In some atavistic way, she was letting things just happen. She could not deny the sexual current . . .

"Mommy, you're not remembering what I said. Pleeeese."

The black rubber head seemed gigantic, circling the small pubic area, cupping the pink inch. The child shivered, exhaling an audible sigh. Then she curled up and nestled into her mother. The mother felt like there was a party of babies at her breast. The child was still and silent.

■

In the moment of passing travail, she felt red and white emotions. Jennifer looked up with a sideways motion of her hand and asked, "Mommy, can I touch your hairy place?" She flipped a mental coin, hoping the penny would take a month to fall.

"How about some cookies?"

"Uh, uh. Can I have another turn?" She decided not to babble or bowdlerize, and summoned her adult and maternal resources.

"Jennifer, my sweet, this game is like birthdays or Christmas, not to happen in bunches."

There was a moment of pause in the child's eyes. Then she catapulted from the bed.

"Well then, dress me."

She ran down the steps and into the yard, tripping over her feet, an angel slipping on wings. From the window, the mother watched the child examine a long-toothed leaf and stick it in her shoe. Jennifer pranced around, singing a funny made-up song. The dog sniffed close behind. She turned around and caught him by the tail. She tried to stick the leaf through his collar. The dog protested. The child insisted.

The mother stood looking out the window. A slight shiver ran through her body as she glanced back at the rumpled bed. She watched the child lift off her feet, skipping. Then Jennifer stopped and looked up at the sky, curious about the cirrus that was moving in.

If there was fault to find, let others find it. At that moment, she felt like a monk among his enchantments.

"THIS CAN HAPPEN

WHEN YOU'RE MARRIED"

THIS CAN
HAPPEN
WHEN
YOU'RE
MARRIED

Karen Chase

You find blue sheets the color of sky with
the feel of summer, they smell like clothes
drying on the line when you were small.
They feel unusual on your skin; you and your husband
sleep on them.

You find thick white towels that absorb a lot
of water. When you come from the bath, you are
cold for a moment, you think of snow for a moment,
you wrap yourself in a towel, dry off the water.

Now, you unpack your silver, after years, polish it,
set it in red quilted drawers your mother lined
for you when you were young.

You and your husband are in bed. The windows are open.
There is a smell from the lawn. It's dark and late. You
and your husband are in the sheets. He is like a horse.
You are like grass he is grazing, you are his field. Or
he's a cow in a barn, licking his calf. It's raining out.

He gets up, walks to the other room. You listen
for his step, his breath. It is late. For moments
before you sleep, you hear him singing.

He comes to bed. He touches your face. He touches
your chin and lips. Later, he tells you this. He puts
his head on your breast. You are dreaming of Rousseau
now, paintings of girls and deserts and lions.

yellow

LIFE WITH THE BRAIN

■

*Joy
Tremewan*

I take off my glasses and look at him. The Brain is across the study, slouching in his easy chair, fondling the curl he always fondles when reading. His glasses make his eyes huge. He is a curly owl.

"You read too much," I say.

He looks at me, startled. We have not spoken for hours. "This from a woman who spends six hours a day reading and four hours a night writing about reading?" he says and grins.

"Well, anyway, I need a bath." I get up and pass by him. Those eyes so large watching me; his nose so large, his lips o so large. The curls, black curls all over his head. He looks at me. Eye contact. Still a shiver up my spine. He looks bewildered, still.

I go to the bathroom and turn on the hot water. The tub is too small. It is the average tub, designed for the average person, by charts, diagrams and polls—all incorporated to please the average bather. I am here with this average tub, thinking, when Brain and I are rich, when the mythical time comes, we will have a special tub made, one that's six feet eight inches, my size with an inch to spare.

I take off my clothes and put on my robe. I go back to the study. Brain is sitting there almost reading, pondering. "I want you to give me a bath, Brain," I say and throw the dry sponge between him and his book.

"Give you a bath?" he says, shocked. I like to shock him.

"Yes, yes, yes. I want to close my eyes and have someone take care of it all, make sure I get clean, make sure I get my teeth brushed, tuck me in and make all the night monsters turn into sleep. I want to be a little girl. Too tired to be a big girl." I go back to the bathroom, drop my robe and ease into the water. It's very hot, my skin turns pink.

I hear Brain's prosthesis tapping on the floor. I relax. He enters. He looks at me, eyes large enough to see all of me; gangly, could've been beautiful if she'd shave or take care of herself—no, those are my thoughts. What does he think? He looks at me. The steam fogs his glasses. He picks up my robe and hangs it on the hook. He puts my clothes in the hamper. He takes off his shirt. It's unusual for him to take off his clothing in the light. Even after five years. His lost leg has made him critical of his whole body; his whole body, boy body, abdomen sloping forward in a curve, regal like David; body hair a light down, boy hair, lean sculpture. I look at him and feel empty. I look at him and feel elated. I should have such a beautiful man sitting in a study with me, sharing a bed with me, raving over books with me; a man who knows so much and will not take his shirt off in the light. Except now. He tries to look casual about it. Slowly he bends down on his knee. He adjusts the prosthesis. I want to jump on him, but I'll knock him over.

He softens the sponge with the soap and hot water. I lean back, close my eyes, and remember.

"His name is Matthew York. He is handicapped and hasn't been able to find work. He lives off Social Security and has lots of time to read. He's one of our few local readers, been a subscriber for six years, thinks we 'review the hell out of the *Times*,' his words. He's available anytime for an interview. By the way, I quit."

The memo was attached to a submitted review of *The Woman Who Lived in a Prologue*. Janis, who left the memo, had called Matthew York and offered him her job. She decided that dedicating a life to reviewing books, then typesetting of the reviews, for what worked out to be a little over minimum wage was a big fat waste. She went to work for an advertising firm that liked her crisp prose and tripled her salary. That left me alone with my little paper, *The Weekly Review*, which was my dream and obsession, and also had a tradition of at least ten book reviews a week. I called Mr. York. I told him there were two requirements for the job: a consuming passion for reading and no desire to become a novelist or poet. He said he'd come for an interview.

When he came into the office I was shocked. He looked

yellow

like a boy. He was shocked by me. I stood nearly a foot over him. "You look like a child," I blurted out. "How old are you?"

He sized me up and said, "I'm sure everyone looks like a child to you. I'm thirty."

I laughed. "It's good you have a sense of humor because I have no social grace. To be even I'll tell you I'm thirty-three. I enjoyed your review of *The Woman Who Lived in a Prologue*. It's one of my favorite books but I never could review it, it set too many emotions floating in me. . . ." So we began to talk, and talk, and talk. Finally he suggested we go for a walk. I noticed his limp. He was telling me about Forche's poetry when he tripped and fell right over. Not knowing what to do, I picked him up and helped him regain balance. He stood there looking shamed and angry; not knowing what to do, I asked, "What's wrong with your leg anyway?"

His eyes flashed, then softened. "I left it behind in a Tupelo hospital. I always thought I could write a good country song—'I left my leg behind, twang, twang, in a Tupelo hospital, twang twang.' A drunk driver got me on my way to school one morning. I was fifteen, going to show off my new bike," he said, not angry, not sad; just words. "So," he said, "you ever play basketball?"

I laughed, "How not? All through school, of course. In college I did some modeling, but that's a sick world; besides, I hate shaving, wearing makeup and competing. I love reading. So I review books and you can have the rest of it."

So we went for coffee, where I bemoaned being a giant, and he listened. Then we went to dinner, where he bemoaned the loss of his leg at an age when emotions are so cruel and short-fused. From dinner we went to his little boarding house room to sleep together in his o so tiny bed. He turned off the lights and took off his clothes, took off his prosthesis, sat on the bed, took off my clothes. His mouth and hands, they put me in flight, like words, like words filling the mind, like exact definitions for every emotion whirling in the heart. Exact motion. All I could think of was, so this is love at first sight.

SILK

■

He runs the sponge in gentle circles up and down my arm and he lifts my arm, sponges and soaps the hair under my arm, slides the sponge over my breast so careful of my nipples, under the breast, over the breast, up to the neck, the back of the neck to the other arm and back to the chest and breasts and down the abdomen, so careful.

We were covered next morning by his blanket. Except my feet. He laughed at me, my feet hanging off the bed like a cartoon. I said, "This room is nothing but books and a desk. You're a real brain, Mr. York!" I began chanting, "Brain, Brain, you're a Brain," and he and I laughed, laughed. He mentioned a poem he'd just read. He jumped from bed on his one leg and hopped to his desk to grab the book. Suddenly he stopped, turned so pale and shamed. He grabbed his long robe, covered himself, hopped back to the end of the bed and turned away from me. I reached for him. He sat still. I put my arm in his robe. My arm circled him easily, his body so smooth in my arms. Yes, I touched where his leg had been, where the skin had grown tight over the end of the bone, where the boy had mended. The remnant of the leg seemed so strong and alone, over and over I ran my hand on Brain's strong leg and then my hand moved slowly as luxury to his penis, which lay bewildered between the two quite different legs, bewildered as if it did not quite believe in this love at first sight I had just discovered. Soon my Brain relaxed, turned towards me. We were words floating in our heads from all the novels, poems we had read in our separate rooms, with our different lonelinesses. He drew the blanket around us. I moaned for him, for the not quite perfect body covering me with perfection in that o so small bed.

Down the abdomen so careful, he runs the sponge, soaping and rinsing. I open my eyes. I see him in my house, the larger

yellow

house, with the larger bed. After five years he looks at me bewildered and he makes love to me in the dark. He soaps my
thighs, and the hair between my legs, and he pours water over
me. He stands and I stand. He follows me to the bedroom. I
kiss him to the bed. I take off his pants. I kiss this boy man, I
take off his prosthesis, he watches, trying to look casual. He
reaches to turn off the lamp. I stop him. I stop him and kiss
his hand.

"Glorie de Dijon.

Crimson.
Starburst."

RAVISHED ON A BED OF ROSES, SKY BY FRAGONARD

■

*Carole
Chambers*

We dragged our mattress out between
the climbing roses
and coupled in the heat of dusk,
two boneless creatures
on the bottom of a different sea.
At last exhausted by the heavy air
and composed for sleep
we played the oldest bed game of them all,
connect the dots of light
and find the intention of the universe.
Consciousness faded with no clue given,
but a small breeze came.

Exhausted by the heavy air
all night the roses showered on us white petals
white petals answered white stars—
intention revealed in the randomness of falling.
We are only falling, we think we're lost.

At sunrise I wakened to the wrangling crows
and a sky of the most tender blue
flocked with little clouds, identical as sheep.
They glowed on the dawn side cream and gold
and on the night side dove grey,
a sky by Fragonard.

yellow

■

A further clue
to the intention of the universe—
the symmetry of form.
I reach for you,
your body roseskin.

SEEDBED
■

Noelle Caskey

On my belly as you enter me,
I think in flowers,
   taste names of roses:

                    Gloire de Dijon.
                    Crimson.
                    Starburst.

SILK

THE ZULU WARRIOR

■

*Jane
Underwood*

I am in high school, maybe younger, when I realize God is a bad joke.

Around this time it occurs to me that either love is also a bad joke or else I have never loved anybody. I decide I have never loved anybody. That means I don't love my parents or brothers or sisters—not that I hate them, I just don't love them, that's all. After high school there is college where I become the girlfriend of my first real boyfriend, Napoleon Goodman, who is a good man indeed. I take ahold of his cock and rub it up and down my clit. Nap can keep it up indefinitely.

There will be a stranger, a man who will see through my sweatshirt today as we pass each other on the trail leading up to the naked lake.

This man will see me and appreciate my Pill-induced breasts in all their largeness. Even now, another man, the strikingly handsome Zulu Warrior, sits in a faraway city imagining my nipples upturned. The image is perfect in his mind. I, in turn, have memorized the slant of his cheeks. We masturbate over the telephone. But the stranger on the path will be sexual in a way I could never foresee, as new men always are. Some detail of his anatomy will mesmerize me. On the way to the lake my hair will shine in the sun, sleek as a twelve-year-old's. I imagine cocks. The morning coffee runs through my bowels and the shit about to come feels sexual.

"I can't stand it anymore in the city," I thought.

The hairdresser had me in the swivel chair and was pressing his cock through tight jeans against my arm. My hair was wet and tangled. He worked the comb through, and I helped him by tugging my head the opposite way to create a perfect tension—thus we constructed a conduit for desire; it ran through the tangles. I heard him catch his breath. There was a shower in the other room. He led me there so I could rinse off

yellow

the fallen hairs. I undressed. He wasn't gay. I live in San Francisco. This was a dream.

It was a Monday.

I made a goal: drink coffee. I was bored, had been bored for weeks. I still remembered how we had fucked, the Stranger and I, in that smoky gray glass booth containing one long-stemmed red rose. Then I reconjured the sensation of the Shy Mechanic's asshole squeezed around my tongue. How I had licked at his nipples! He was very shy on our first date, so I was taken aback when he said, "I just can't stop thinking about licking your clit." I liked him most because he never gave me unasked for advice.

I was thinking of my Shy Mechanic, his smooth chest, how it felt against my face.

But sometimes one man gets superimposed on another. Thus the Zulu Warrior appeared naked and whispering that he wanted to get it in me from behind. He always told me when he was about to come. I pushed my ass against his thighs, telling him to get it in deeper, deeper. He is black, his skin the color of pecans, his hair softly Afroed, and almost seven feet tall. We were using natural birth control—checking mucus and taking temperature. He loved sticking the basal thermometer up my cunt and did it every day. No matter where I was, he pulled down my panties and stuck it up me. I began to crave this.

I wanted men to bring me flowers and hated the ones who did.

That's an exaggeration. But the only flower I ever almost cried over was the wild rose tied to my doorknob, compliments of the Zulu Warrior. He left it for me on his way to see another woman; I didn't know that at the time. Later he brought me strawberries and wine, then lifted the folds of my gown and began to lick my pussy on the livingroom floor. When I thought he was finished, he wasn't; he took me to the bedroom and told me to lie on my back and do it, explaining how such a sight would excite him. I fell instantly in love.

■

I was living in the Castle.

That was the name of the turreted Victorian rooming house. Only two other people lived on my floor—Abdul and Juan. Abdul always pissed on the toilet seat—I never wanted to know him. Juan had hot Latin blood and every weekend went out with a different gorgeous woman, both of them dressed fit to kill. I wasn't averse to his body or his style, just his personality. One day we went for a drive in his new car and smoked a joint. He said hey, how about a movie? I said no, I had plans to meet Napoleon back at the Castle. He said well then, how about a quick dip in the hot tubs? I had never been to the hot tubs, so I agreed. I didn't know I'd have to undress, alone, in front of him, in a room with a door that had a sign saying DO NOT DISTURB. When we arrived we were shown to our room. Juan went down the hall to the toilet and said he would be right back. I should have taken off my clothes right then and jumped into the tub, but when he returned, he found me still standing rooted to the spot, unable to speak. In the silence he began to take off all his clothes. I knew I had to do something—I began to unbutton my blouse. As I removed my clothes, he stood naked under the shower, getting a hard-on. In the tub I wrapped my legs around his waist, and his lips felt very hot. In the sauna he fucked me on the redwood bench, and my cunt felt like lava. An hour later, I met Napoleon for dinner.

Tending flowers on the back porch helps, or washing the floor by hand.

But horseback riding bareback and naked erases the city completely. I do it whenever I can. Usually I go alone. Sometimes I take a lover. We ride naked until our genitals dance and pound. Not everybody can ride horses in the Napa hills. Whores confirm the body too, in their own way. After we stop riding we walk the animals, sweating. I bring berries or pie on these days—cherries, strawberries, or blackberries, rhubarb pie.

yellow

The Stranger walks beside me with a hard-on. I stoop to kiss it, then walk on. When he's had enough of my teasing, he approaches me quickly from the rear and abruptly shoves it up me. I like being made to gasp with renewed virginal shock. My core, if he can reach it, is forever that of a young girl. My embroidery of sexual experience can be unraveled.

My Shy Mechanic had been coming to see me regularly.

But this was our last night together before he left for good. I slid pressing over his body, slid over him, and when he gripped my ass I let it be his and loved how he took what was his. The ragas ran through us as he rubbed oiled hands over my breasts. Our skins glowed with lanternlight. I arched in to brush my lips across the inside of his neck. His hands ran from my thighs to shoulders, in sleep we lay like two warm lakes lapping into each other. Now that he's gone I reconstruct each touch. Under cold gray skies repressing rain, the City lies in wait.

All night I promised them I would do their breasts in time for Christmas.

Since I had never sculpted a thing in my life, I walked around nude, in order to bolster my confidence, always aware of my full and inviting tits. I took photographs of the ones they had in mind. I was afraid to work from real life. On the day before Christmas I still hadn't begun; my pleasure, however, at learning to walk around unselfconsciously nude and sensual overshadowed any worry of failing as a sculptor.

More than anything else I wanted to know what I wanted.

I also wanted the Zulu Warrior. If only I could get him alone, in some isolated doorway, pull down his pants and suck him off! He wouldn't be so inclined to give me lectures on logic then. The only thing in the world that made me ecstatically happy were the moments when I realized the emotional power I had over him. Unfortunately this power was useless unless we were together. He knew this and saw me less and less. Such confidence scared him. Fortunately, I never loved him for his courage.

■

Waking up alone in the mornings drove me to panic and despair.

I vowed to begin a new adventure. I would pursue the only man I'd ever known longer than one lifetime. The gray cat played with a cherry on the cream-colored floor. As the vodka ran through my veins my Womanhood surged. I wanted his baby. I wanted it before I turned thirty. My womb began to open. The wall of my vagina knew I was serious. The sperm in his balls started chomping at the bit. The Zulu Warrior and I were hundreds of miles apart.

The more I worked the less I wanted to work.

I either had to find a meaningful job or come up with a cause. I was manic depressive, which complicated matters even more. One hour I desperately needed a psychiatrist, the next hour the psychiatrist needed me. Conflict was my most natural mode of being—we all have our paths. I went over to the Stranger's house bearing plums, vodka and artichoke hearts. The plums were ripe, the vodka Russian, the artichokes mysterious. We listened to jazz. Once I looked at his bed but quickly averted by eyes when I caught him noticing the direction of my glance. I tried to hint at my vulnerabilities without appearing too vulnerable. I alluded to my sexual past, emphasizing the exotic. I sat on the ledge above the heater with my legs spread, letting the heat rise into my crotch. I tried to visualize him sitting on the floor beside me, then reaching out to touch me there. Time passed until the heat got to be too much. He adjusted the light over the drafting table. I went to the kitchen, rinsed out the artichoke bowl, came back, put the cap on the vodka and reached for my jacket. It was obvious— either we were too much alike or too different. I couldn't figure out which, but what did it matter? That night I pissed into the aluminum mixing bowl beside my bed.

Sex is an inspiration. Inspiration is a state of grace.

One minute I wanted to die, the next minute inspiration swept over me—and in it appeared the possibility of total

yellow

rearrangement. I relived my face hugging the belly of the Shy Mechanic. We'd clung to each other like that, not moving, for those long minutes that get measured in heartbeats. The smell of him and the touch of his belly against my cheek set my cunt to pulsing in slow preparation to be fucked a second time. I put my face down low, my mouth around his cock. He reached around with his leg, put his foot on my cunt and pressed into my hole with his heel. I moaned in pleasure, loving his mastery. In a whisper, as he came, he called out my name, and the sound of my own name coming out of the strange wilderness that was his voice excited me even more. I drew him in deeper.

When I go to his house my pleasure makes me shy.

The Stranger has no shirt on. My hair brushes his cheek. The slit in my lavender top invites him to touch the edge of my breast. I want to be soft. I want his arms to not stop holding me even though I know they will. I want to be softly strapped down and made to do things. Clouds move past tall city buildings. They should be in the desert, majestic, not wedged inbetween. Red electric digitals etch out time. I doubt that men and women ever get tired of touching each other, the same endless touches.

I wanted to surrender. I seldom surrender.

He swept me up in his arms. I wanted to fuck and be fucked. As soon as I walked in the door he saw the woman under the cotton shirt and terrycloth socks. He saw the goddess. I wanted to be a goddess. I surrendered.

Passion is when two people let the coffee boil.

Indirectly passion has to do with buying a new pair of shoes or wearing a necklace. The Stranger and I have been taunting each other, and I move toward the trip to get new shoes. When I lean over the tub to check the running water, he stands behind me, pressing his cock against my ass, coming close, then moving away, then coming close again. I run my hands through the water. I'm wet. My breasts dangle and he reaches out to cup them. Have I really become a grown-up woman? I feel flushed as he spreads my thighs, begins to finger me.

SILK

■

Now that I have become optimistic I feel pessimistic.

The Stranger enters, suggesting I run naked into the ocean. He has an erection, but we lie together perfectly still. A current of energy flows through our genitals so strong that orgasm is inevitable even without movement. Suddenly the Zulu Warrior appears, stroking my forehead, telling me, "Don't worry, come to bed." He massages my shoulders. We fuck in a New Mexico desert. I am passionately independent, passionately dependent. I laugh because it feels so good. We are in each other's minds even across the years and miles.

The baby grand was poised beside the front window, and in the dining room cookies, cakes and plums awaited us.

I spied the bottle of sparkling burgundy. Our hostess had only one eye and wore fashionable heels. She was married to her childhood sweetheart. I wondered how often they made love. During the recital the Stranger reached around, slid his hand down the front of my blouse. I smiled. He had a hard-on. We probably should have taken our leave, but I was hungry for a marble fudge bar. While wandering in the backyard afterwards, we discovered a tiny guest house nestled beneath a tree of pink flowers. Inside this house was a single bed, a chair and a barrel with an ashtray on top containing five cigarette butts. Since there was no one else in the backyard, he began to goose me.

The Zulu Warrior gets me hot, walks me to the door, pats my ass, sends me out to fuck another man.

I go, fuck, keep the come inside, hurry back. As soon as I walk in the door he pulls down my panties to see my wet bush, come dripping down my thighs smelling like fresh bread. He licks it. Yes, I'm wet with another man. He likes this, fills me up again.

The Conga Player eyes me.

Genitals stir across the distance. Somehow we will connect, fuck and part.

254

Yellow

■

The first time I met him I was swinging in a hammock.

He came out his front door. I was swinging in a hammock reading a book. He came out his front door, walked past me, left a breeze of himself behind. I was swinging in the hammock, he came out his front door, walked past me, stopped to talk, looked at my body, wanted me unconsciously, said, "Let's get together sometime," walked away. Later we shared beer. His breath rippled the tiny hairs on my neck as he leaned over my shoulder. Lust light as a feather entered my nape. We had, it was clear, karma to share. We were not spiritually very evolved. We had lust. Later he brought wine. I touched his cock through his pants, bent down to kiss him there, promising everything with my eyes. He wanted to fuck me right away. I refused him—my Zulu Warrior.

Opened my mouth, took him to bed, sucked him off 'til he moaned, "Shit oh woman!"

Took him to my bed. Sucked him off 'til he got hard against my ass, hard against the crack of my ass. The tip of his cock pressed hot against me, pushing gently, asking, pushing, pushing, plying me open. He said RELAX JUST RELAX I'LL BE GENTLE I'M GONNA FUCK YOU UP THE ASS, COME UP YOUR ASS, UP YOUR SWEET LITTLE ASS YOUR HOT LITTLE ASS YOUR HOT WHITE LITTLE ASS YOU BITCH OOOOOOH I'M GONNA HOLD YOUR TITS WHILE I COME . . . I'M COMING NOW I'M COMING OOOOOOOH THAT'S IT. yeah.

Gobble gobble chomp chomp bloody guts and egg whites.

Intestinal lumps. That old man on TV rules India, drinks his piss every day. Sodomy is good for you. I will cut off the priest's ears, strip for you in the living room, spread the crack of my ass, beg you to fuck me there, and in the mouth, and in my face. THE THING THAT TURNS ME ON MORE THAN ANYTHING ELSE IS REMEMBERING THE TIME YOU SAID YOU WANTED TO HOLD ME, JUST HOLD ME.

SILK

The first time we kissed, how malleable the Caveman's lips were, so warm.

Now we're platonic and he's giving me shitfaced advice once more. But later he'll come to my bed, wanting me. I'll acquiesce, taking him between my legs, his cock so big I'll remember how scared I was the first time I saw it. In the morning, as he moans, I'll grip it. He says we don't share love. His eyes see well into others but not into himself. When I look at them, I feel a painful sensation. I live two blocks from the bar. Sometimes, after having had many beers, he remembers me.

I don't want to work eight hours a day for money.

I bought a lacy bra; it shows off my nipples, hooks in the front. Last night a man knocked on my door. I wasn't home. He went to a phone booth and called me, as if he didn't believe I was gone. It sounded like a Volkswagen when he drove off. Who was he? The Volkswagen Man. Did he want to fuck me? I want sex, I want power. I don't give a shit about fashion. I could work fulltime and make twenty thousand and go on a three-week vacation. Did he drive madly to my house, obsessed with the fantasy of fucking me? I have put on the rice, fed the cat. I wear glass-spiked high heels at the party, dance madly while men watch my black-seamed stockings. My black dress is dotted with flesh and lavender. It fits tight over my stomach, and the hairs in my armpits are just asking to be tugged at.

Stuff fish into my mouth, and chicken and potatoes and chocolate.

When he was in the shower I pulled down my panties, sat on the toilet, was halfway through a piss when he stepped out with a hard-on, one I wanted to touch. He yawned a sexy moan as he stretched out his arms and his cock shot up. The last of my piss trickled down. I asked him to wipe me. He did, then straddled me on the toilet seat. I pissed just a little bit more. He got even harder. We fucked on the toilet. He told me to take a shit and moved his cock inside me slowly as I did.

yellow

■

Let's just be friends.

Oh what the hell, fuck me, I'm quivering. Let's sleep in separate beds. Oh what the hell, let's just fuck all night. Fuck it, let's drive to the beach. I'll take off my jeans and run through the waves while you watch, wanting me, not wanting me, in my sexy-lady hat, wide-brimmed straw hat from Ecuador, banded in black lace. Don't touch me. I want to fuck you. Put your finger up my cunt as I sit open to the tide coming in and the waves washing over us.

I stood on the edge of the freeway. It turned into a long lake.

I undressed, took off the gray sweatshirt, the black lace panties. As the men drove by I was removing the smokey stockings, had one of them rolled down to mid-calf. Their macho whistles contained such awe I could not become angry. Soon I was naked, ready for a swim. The Zulu Warrior sat beside me on the water's edge. I jumped in first. He watched as I came up with wet hair tangled over my eyes. I began to swim. When I came up he was beside me in the water. One small black hair grew out from beside my nipple. He said it was beautiful and that it excited him greatly.

The Zulu Warrior and I are insane.

An empty hotel room with one window behind a sheer curtain, empty wine bottle on the sill, will soon explode from the fullness of our touching.

I am in high school. Maybe younger. When I realize God is a bad joke.

Around this time it occurs to me that either love is also a bad joke or I have never loved anybody. I decide I have never loved anybody. Once the Caveman fucked a prostitute in Amsterdam and came nine times. I think she knew some trick.

"Flecked with earth

with earth

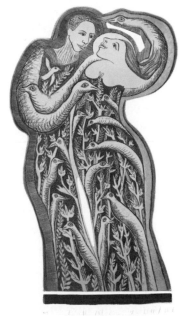

And Needles of Pine"

AFTER LOVE-MAKING

■

Jeffery Beam

After rain
pigeons roost in the vines
A wet fortress their beds
I want to struggle to be good with them
cooing and damp in their blue tails

ORGANIC GARDENING

■

Ira Wood

Everyone else I know accepts temporary malaise, the blues, as an ordinary human infirmity like the flu and sees nothing wrong with a few lackluster days of self-pampering and doughy lying about. But my own chosen love, my Cynthia, the caramel center of my bittersweet life, views depression as indistinguishable from masturbation and weight lifting: a waste of limited male energy.

I admit it. The tides of my disposition fluctuate with my luck at the mail box. Following this morning's letter of rejection I returned to the house with the glazed, magnetized eyes of the children of the damned.

"Uh oh," was all Cynthia said.

"Maybe it's a sign. Maybe I should give up playwriting. Finally admit it. No, I do not have any talent. It's time I grew up, accepted the fact that some people have it and some people never will."

She waited for me to finish. It is no secret that in her women's group I am know as Uncle Vanya.

yellow

"Maybe I should just give up and find something I'm good at."

"How about pottery? Or the guitar," she said. "Definitely. The guitar. And give yourself a solid month. Then if the Rolling Stones don't ask you to join them, take up, let's see, sand painting." According to Cynthia you don't pout about rejections, you make more submissions, just like you don't jerk off when you can make love or bench press dumbbells when you can work in your garden.

Which is what we are doing, pulling summer beets, red and hard and clinging with earth, raking over the soil and planting cabbage in their place. Our bodies are machines, oiled with perspiration dusted brown. I pull a beet, Cynthia will take it. She shovels manure, and then I rake it. Rake it, take it, rake it, take it, on and on and on. I do not feel like talking and Cynthia obliges me. She knows, the work is my cure.

Cynthia's legs are caked with socks of earth, her forehead bears an airbrush smudge where she whisked her hair from her eyes. She wears a tight-fitting tank top, only a film that breathes with her sweat slippery breasts, and a pair of terry cloth shorts, damp in the crotch where they ride. I have not lost my desire for her. Our good sex is my only pleasure, and perhaps the only reason she merely sighs when our eyes meet, sighs with a resigned shake of the head which says, I'll wait.

With the planting finished we sit, ankles crossed, under the land's oldest white oak and cut the beets from their greens. Hummingbirds thrash desperately, sipping nectar in flight as our black sentries, the crows, gather in the branches. Her gaze does not leave me, my soft belly that hangs over my shorts like the yeasty overspill of a muffin, my thick haunches, the odd patches of hair on my shoulders and neck. I am beautiful to her. Not almost beautiful if I lost ten pounds, not potentially respectable if I finally had a play produced, but unreservedly beautiful for who I am.

Our toes dig the loamy soil, our cat wreathes our ankles in pensive figure eights. The satin leaves of the Swiss chard, the castle wall of scarlet runner beans, the tomatoes, drooping pregnant with fruit, all wait.

She draws my face to hers. Her fingers skim the line of my cheek and fan wide at my neck and shoulders. Her palms slide across my nipples. As I raise her arms to slip off her damp top, her breasts, streaked with grit, tumble against my chin. Our bodies are wet, smelling of sweat and work, flecked with earth and needles of pine. As she pulls my shorts to my knees I kick them free of my ankles and ease onto a soft mattress of damp hay.

Drinking one another, sliding, licking, our noises are quieter than the catbirds calling and the passionate orchestra of crickets in the grass. Cynthia swings on top of me and places me inside her and we clutch, barely breathing, just feeling, not moving, murmuring, both of us, with our own primal sounds. How grateful we are.

My best friend laughs at my gardening. Why bother? You can buy the same damned lettuce at the Safeway. Old people garden. And spinsters. Farmers and immigrants. But he doesn't know. He has no idea.

Picture standing, naked, ankle deep in the earth, with your love. In July, when the air is a dense wet aura, a flannel sheet grazing your bare skin; when the squirrels are so busy they forget the bird feeders, when moths, like pellets, bat your windows and the prickly fronds of summer squash tickle your inner thighs. You have watched your love kneeling, stretching, tugging weeds. Her muscles slide beneath her skin. She sweats where your tongue wants to be. And the good air fills you, and your body thrums from the inside out. You are an animal, naked in the grass, in the dirt. You are hot and you want.

(There would be more gardens in America, I think, if *Organic Gardening* or *Country Journal* popularized the notion of garden sex. Plant your bed and sleep in it. Make your love and eat it, too. Sloganeering aside, a muscular pair of thighs behind a rake is a bigger turn-on than a pair of sixteen-year-old buns sewn into a pair of designer jeans. Any day.)

yellow

Always an outsider, in the garden I am at the center. Not a hub about which all else turns, but an organ breathing life inside a great whole. In the garden my body eclipses my mind's poor potential for pleasure, my tension spills in a tide of orgasm and my love and I, bodies braided, lips licking salty skin, twine and roll like dolphins, float weightless on a crackling hill of straw.

A GOOD SIGN

*Ronald
Baatz*

she comes into the office in the morning
at the motel and she hands me the book of
chinese poems she borrowed nearly a year ago.
i'm genuinely happy to see her though and i
throw my arms around her, and when i do i think
she displays about the same amount of happiness
when she throws her arms around me. where this
happiness has come from i'm sure is just as much
a mystery to her as it is to me, considering we've
only spent a single night together, and that was
around a year ago, right around the time i lent her
the book of poems. i'm not on duty, so we go for
a long walk on the road that goes up and around and
out of town by the reservoir. it's a blowy, turbulent
autumn day, and we're both bundled up in winter coats.
conversation is slightly erratic, sometimes approaching
the awkward side, but by some precious small miracle
it manages to purr along well enough. when i look
at her i can't help but to think of the recent women
in my life, the miniature uncaring affairs, and i
wonder whether we can ever have anything any better.
perhaps she is wondering this very same question.
i cannot tell. how many men have i seen her around
town with? my god, there have been a few. our
stroll takes us into the woods where we come to
sit on a long log, which because of rot is very
soft, very comfortable. as we sit there we kiss,
slowly, mixing in few words, but that's as far as

yellow

it goes. and after a while i have to get up and
take a pee off further in the woods. i'm a
stickler for my privacy when i pee outside.
as i stand there i try to figure out my bearings
with this woman, struggling for some clue
that might tip me off as to which direction
we might be going in. when i turn to see
how she's doing i see her squatting in the
leaves also peeing. this i take as being a
good sign.

"*I* HAVE

BeeN THere"

JANUSCZ

■

*Elaine Perez
Zickler*

Januscz came after Bert, Bert was after Ron, and Ron was first. I don't know if thinking about things helps or not. Of course, it does in advance. But, how is it possible to think about love in advance of when it happens? It's equally impossible to think about it at the time it's happening and when it's all over, what's the point? Except to feel a little good, a little sad, a little soft, a little weepy. Januscz was the oldest man I ever loved, not counting my father. But, of course, I never loved my father the way I loved Januscz. And it was impossible to have thought about loving him ahead of time. It never occurred to me that I could ever love a man that old that way.

Whenever I think of Januscz now, I think of the two of us sitting in my kitchen. He's sitting at the table with a cup of coffee in front of him. He has a cup and saucer and spoon in front of him and he is dressed in his suit, only his shirt is opened at the neck and his tie is folded on the table next to his place setting. Januscz was a little heavy, but not fat. Just solid and mature looking. He was nearly sixty, but I could never imagine him looking any different either before or after that time in his life. He had no baby pictures, of course, no pictures of himself at all until he was a young man, until after the war when he was here in the States, but even those pictures show this same solid, mature-looking, sad-looking man. Oh, and I forgot the cigarette. Always the cigarette. Just there, rolling around between his fingers and his thumb, occasionally putting one out in the ashtray only to thoughtfully light another with the next move of his hand. Januscz was certainly a romantic man, I thought and still do. But I could not say why I thought this precisely. It had to do with his sitting in that kitchen chair while I stood pouring coffee or frying him an egg or chopping vegetables for soup.

Januscz never came out of the bedroom at all until the two

YELLOW

boys had left the house, on those mornings after he had stayed all night. He came down fully dressed and so did I, except for my shoes or for a bra under my sweater. Usually I dressed in a skirt and a sweater. He seemed to like my red sweater best, especially when I wore it over nothing at all. My red sweater and my plaid wool skirt and my bare feet in the kitchen and my hair just pulled back so it didn't fall into his eggs or soup. Januscz never told me what he liked, but he trained me by looks and smiles; his sad, averted face could make me do or be almost anything at all for him. It was the least I could do for him, considering what he had lost. Everything was all. He had lost everything in the war: parents, siblings, relatives, proofs, records, possessions, even his nationality itself—they were Estonian—had been utterly lost, destroyed. Only Januscz survived. And Januscz somehow made his sad and aristocratic way into my life after Ron left it, after Bert left it, at the time when my boys were getting ready to leave it, after I had accepted the fact that I might never leave this old house that Bert had left me in. Sometimes, I felt like my great-great-great-great-grandmother in Virginia must have after the Civil War, never having counted on getting older myself, never having counted on certain things quietly changing whether I was listening or not. By the time I met Januscz I had forgotten why I asked Ron to leave and why he had left so willingly. What difference did it make? I had forgotten why I had thought Bert could change my life for me and that mattered even less, to my surprise.

All I knew was that scene in the kitchen after a night together was a photograph I would have liked taken for me. Who could have taken it just as I'm telling it, so that I was moving between Januscz and the sink or Januscz and the stove or Januscz and the refrigerator and my skirt was moving around my naked calves and my breasts were moving under my red woolen sweater and he was looking down at his coffee or with his hands holding the cigarette in a gesture of prayer looking out the window at the house across the driveway? And the day is early winter, after Christmas, and it is sunny and the light is white and pale blue coming in the window and Januscz will never drink coffee from a mug but only from cup and saucer although he has never said this to me but I know and so for the first time in years I am using the pink rose-patterned Limoges that my grandmother left to me and for the first time in my marriage the silver spoons are washed every day and the Czechoslovakian linen napkins are ironed every week. None of this did I do, or would I have done, for Ron even, and especially, if he had asked it of me.

And I would stop by his side and try to see what he was seeing out the window. Nothing. A bird at the feeder. A cardinal, perhaps. The male like a sudden splash of blood moving through the white and blue air. Or the female, dull and drained except for the blush of her beak. The woman next door, a divorce lawyer, getting into her battered car. And as I stood next to him and we both looked out together, not at each other, his hand would set down his cup, or unlock itself from its prayerful jointure, and move under my sweater toward my breast, or under my skirt, sadly and unlustfully feeling for my body as if to merely reassure itself of its presence there. Yes. A breast. Two breasts and nipples which wrinkle and harden into knots even before they are touched, even as the first drift of cold kitchen air slips under my sweater ahead of his hand. And yes, a vulva, two sets of lips and a hungry mouth which salivates in anticipation, like a baby drooling and groping blindly for the breast when its cheek is only brushed by its mother's hand. And we could go on or not from there. I could sit on his lap, facing him, but with my gaze fixed on the scene outside the window sill, while he moved his penis inside me. Quietly. Quietly. Like refugees. Like escapees. Or he could only feel. Two breasts. Two nipples. Two sets of lips. Counting. Accounting for all my parts. Feeling with fingers, not exactly proprietary, but appreciative and secretive. All there. Good.

yellow

All there. And some day, perhaps, everything will be returned, restored to its proper place. For now, he checks the secret hiding places for the few things he has managed to secret away. And for now, they are there.

With Januscz, it seemed that all the foolish parts of me were transformed into something tender and fragile and precious, like that old china Ron hated and Bert would have replaced with something sturdier, uglier, more handmade-looking. What I had had to distort for Ron and Bert in various ways, silly, childlike, flashy, whatever, Januscz wanted purely for itself. Whatever Ron and Bert had required, I had managed some facsimile of, never quite consciously. And it wasn't as if I was trying to please them so much as to keep them. Pleasing them, I realize now, would have been impossible, but honorable as a goal. And so, I pleased Januscz in whatever ways I could perceive or devise. And his pleasure was my pleasure. And my pleasure was as intense as it was silent and continuous in his presence. All of life when he was in my life was charged with an energy I cannot reduce to sex, but perhaps if I changed the perspective or the balance so that I could convey how every action became expanded into sex, by our sex, then perhaps I would come close to telling it.

That was the sitting in the kitchen, the moving back and forth between Januscz and the food and the utensils and the appliances and looking out with Januscz and it was in that seamless way Januscz was inside me the next minute or touching me under my sweater and skirt. The rhythm of our life together, the way that every act and movement and per-formance was transformed by the . . . what? I don't know how to say it. The space of our intercourse, let's say. Normally, this space is very small; the bed, the night time, the space taken up by the penis in the vagina, the tongues in the mouths, had expanded, as if blown up and enveloping us. Within this thick fluidity we moved in perpetual rhythms of intercourse. There was not a glance, not a gesture, not a word that did not enter into the transitivity of our world together.

"Helen. Helena." He spoke my name into my ear, into my neck, into my navel. He moved into me and out of me all night on those nights when he stayed with me. It was in no way the athletic performance of a young man, of Ron or Bert, as they marathoned, raced, climbed, scored over and through my body, then headed for the showers or the refrigerator or collapsed like Jason or Daniel after a hard day of play. No. This was the two of us together, unable to separate, uninterested in goals, in endings, intent on the thing itself. Coming was what we got out of the way immediately. And then it was the repetition of the movement itself that we each, sadly, distressingly found to be each other's greatest need and hunger. Insatiable. Impossible. He must push me away and then bind me to him. Both. Both. It was in the loss and recovery of our bodies, repeated finally in every minuscule act of daily life, that we found our existences together. And so we were mostly silent. Only, "Helen. Helena." And "Januscz." As if to try to establish thus, some polarity, some solidity in this liquidity that was our love.

Januscz went away to work like any other man. Ron was a doctor, a surgeon, and had been gone most of the time. When he was home, he tended to be like a man on vacation, intent on grabbing some distraction, some entertainment in a short time. Busy at leisure, impatient with leisurely feelings like depression or despair, not introspective at all, he watched games on TV or concentrated on buying a shore house for a long stretch of time, which we then furnished and scheduled our lives around for several warm months a year. Friends came over and we ate dinners and the men shot baskets or we all skiied together on winter weekends. When Ron left, after I asked him to leave, I stayed in the house for a while, then settled for this old house under Bert's influence. The wisdom of it is that it was so

yellow

inexpensive I have no mortgage to keep; otherwise, it's just an old house in need of repairs I can't afford to make. Under Bert's influence I also relinquished or renounced certain financial arrangements with Ron that at the time seemed crass, punitive, and unnecessary; now, I know I will be a little poor for the rest of my life. The boys will be fine. They still ski and go to the beach house and will go to fine colleges as planned. Only I, by choice it seems, will live on the edge from now on.

Bert never worked regularly at outside jobs, but he worked nevertheless. He made a start at fixing up this house, but as he considered life and work to be inseparable, he never planned to finish anything he began and when he left me he also left off working on the house. Januscz, like my father, went away to a job and returned home again when it was finished, when the day was finished. He was too aristocratic by nature to identify himself by work or profession; like any poor man he knew that working was for eating, but not for living. One lived at home if one was lucky, if one had love there.

And so, Januscz's goings and comings were punctual and resigned, unadorned by pretensions, unrelieved by philosophy. He didn't talk much about his work to me or anyone else. He was not a poor man, however. I realize I have compared him to a poor man, but I meant only that he had a poor man's attitude toward work. In reality, he was a successful businessman who, nevertheless, did not pretend to love his work, or to be a better person because of it. There was something else always at work in Januscz, I thought. But, perhaps it was only my extreme tendency to romanticize. After all, it was I who had glorified Ron's work as a calling at first and it was I who had been ecstatic about Bert's worship of the commonplace, his ability to elevate the most menial task into something worshipful. Even now, I can see that there were these men in my life doing things and there was I busily weaving tales about them, tales they never even heard or read anywhere. And about Januscz,

SILK

the tale is that nothing mattered to him as much as our life together, our love. He, like I, perceived his goings and comings as goings and comings from and to me.

I need to explain somehow what I can only call the sense of detail which marks, for me, my life with Januscz. Perhaps this is not meaningful at all because everyone, after all, has this sense of detail. Every life is nothing but detail. So boring it can be. So tedious and routine that the details no longer are noticeable, like a relief work that has been rubbed flat by years of exposure, friction, weather. And then detail can be everything, can be irritating like so many children's voices shouting for attention at once. Me and me and me without let-up. It's so funny I'm realizing all at once that my sense of detail with Januscz was exactly what I sensed Bert was trying for, but never getting. And his gross failure was what made him so funny to me, so fatally funny all the time. This is it, then. With Januscz, the details became important, everything, and utterly unremarked. He did not call attention to them constantly the way Bert did; nor did he obliterate them the way Ron did. Rather, he lived in them like a man, which is precisely what he was, who has found again something that had surely died. There is no question that it has died, is dead, has been dead and yet lives. In the china cup and saucer, in the silver fork and spoon, in the ivory damask Czechoslovakian linen table napkins, in the vegetable borscht, in my breasts, in between my legs. He touched and tasted all of it with great attention, silent and reverent and appreciative and solemn. Like a patient stone worker or archeologist, he extricated the details of daily life from their flattened or buried lives and restored them to themselves. Here a spoon, a cup, a woman's hair tied back. Notice the strands of her hair, the heft of her breasts under her loose red sweater, how weight and gravity are hinted at and delightfully, incongruously opposed to her slightness, her petite height and the thinness of her fingers and ankles. I began to think of myself this way under Januscz's steady gaze, his

yellow

discovering hands. I began to pay attention to myself as a marvelous play of detail, a place where forces had struggled to achieve a balance for all of my life, it seemed, and required only his gaze, his hands, to affirm such balance.

My breasts, for example, had been a source of crisis and ambivalence for all my life. If I really think about them, and I did for the first time with Januscz, I must think back to my mother's breasts and even to my grandmother's breasts and must include the fact that my happiness at the birth of first one son and then another included a great relief that they would never have breasts. This initial and, as I have come to realize, sad triumph waned over the years 'til, by the time I knew Januscz, I longed for that daughter I could never have, and yearned for those breasts again. When he gazed at me and touched me, my breasts seemed to claim their past and mourn for their future; suddenly, they were my grandmother's breasts that had nursed my mother for so many years she could re-member them into her own middle and old age and sit next to me and talk about them in such a way that I felt waves of yearning, envy and anger, like a starving child listening to a description of someone's feasting. She, for so many reasons, had not used her own breasts for nursing. She was modern and busy and her first husband, my father, apparently could not tolerate such an extended maternal life for her body. He wanted it all over with and she had been happy to oblige him, she said. She got her figure back in no time. Of course, I had nursed both Jason and Daniel for as long as they seemed to want it and had felt a vicarious pleasure during that time, had felt, in fact, a yearning for my own breasts and an occasional pang of envy for their own greedy sucking, never stopping until they rolled off the nipple in stupors, and the last mouthful of my milk overflowed their puckered little lips. I would kiss it from their mouths, the taste of myself, but only in utter solitude.

SILK

Increasingly with Januscz, those moments which were previously moments of shame, of solitude, of private joy and loneliness, emerged and could be shared with him. And the remarkable, the utterly remarkable and solitary pursuits of a body that had been exposed, certainly, in one way or another all of my life, but never truly shared, became unremarked and revered in Januscz's way. How can I say what it was like to pursue a pleasure, like that taste of my own warm, sweet, thin milk from my infant son's mouth, an infantile pleasure, to its end and to do it with the solemnity and dignity that Januscz brought to all of life, especially to the life of the body? How can I assure anyone that there was not one moment of embarrassment, or pride, or striving, or masquerading, or numb boredom, or fear, or loathing, or disgust in our life together? How could I convince my friends, especially Ruth, who knows me so well, that Januscz was the first man I ever knew, with the possible exception of my father, who loved women? And to be truthful, I would have to except my father from that category because, although he loved me, he didn't love my mother the way Januscz loved me. He couldn't have, or everything in my life would have been different. All of it. Changed utterly.

Perhaps Ruth, but certainly not Emma, who cannot imagine the sadness of others, it seems, and particularly not mine, could imagine that Januscz and I had cried together. Wept. Naked. For all those bad feelings we did not feel for, or with, each other, all the ones I have listed, sadness compensated. Januscz was always sad, especially when he was happy, when he was fully in his pleasure. Then he was most likely to weep. And again, I cannot help comparing and contrasting, as if I were still a freshman at Bryn Mawr. But it was one more thing, one more difference with Januscz, this weeping we did. With Ron, there was weeping at the end for him. And it seemed to seal our separation and divorce more firmly than anything else had done, as if I had driven him to

yellow

the one act that was beyond reparation. Or, it was more that I had seen him weeping so abjectly and it was this being seen, finally, that he could never live down. My weeping had been trivial, baby's tears, all of it. Loneliness. Separation. Pain of dislocation. Pain of exhaustion when the boys were both babies. Pain of childbirth. All of it he had enjoyed in a certain way from his position of strength, from his distance, from his bemused masculinity. I have heard men say, then and now, that crying was a kind of luxury that women could indulge in but men could not. Men envied women this ease and relief, I have heard. But, with Ron, even if I granted him the envy, it was clear that the acquisition, finally, of this one luxury he had ostensibly denied himself all his life with me, did not gratify so much as it shamed and humiliated and angered him beyond repair. Bert never cried at all, publicly or privately, I am certain. He considered my tears as well as my rages to be expressions of weakness from which he recoiled in a kind of horror. He was a man who moved me to violence. If I had set myself to the task of making him cry, I'm sure I would have had to kill him first.

Januscz wept in such a purposeful way. It was not to get sympathy or to stop an argument; it was simply to express his sadness. He wept when he spoke about his parents and his childhood and curiously, it was such a relief that he could weep that it foreclosed on any sympathy he may have demanded, justifiably, from me. He sympathized with himself, with his own lost past, with his own little boy that he was. He didn't ask this of anyone else, especially of me. But, I hear the objections. I hear Ruth especially saying, but, there you are. The audience he needs. Of course he is demanding. He is demanding with every word he utters. All I can say in his defense, in my own defense, is that Januscz wept for the impossibility of sympathy: he wept because nothing could be done except weeping. Even if I wept with him, for my own losses more than his, that was as much as I could ever give him in compensation, and he never asked for it. Januscz asked for certain things, for china cups and silver spoons and linen napkins, and these I was able and only too happy to give to him.

He was neither kind nor unkind to my friends. It was I who sensed that they made him uncomfortable and were, in turn, uncomfortable with us. Ruth continued to drop by in the old way for coffee, but could not bear to sit at the kitchen table with Januscz while I stood and walked back and forth between the stove and the sink and the table. I, for my part, could not manage to sit at the table with her when he was there. It was very awkward. He remained silent, refusing to speak because he had nothing to say to her. She, for her part, stared at him the way she does and I could hear her thinking, well, fuck you then, I also find you not worth the expense of words. More painfully, I could also hear her wondering what he was doing in my kitchen, of all places. In any logical world, he would have been in hers. She was exactly the woman for him in most ways, and I was not. Even Emma, with her morose fixation on her unhappy childhood and her fears of losing Martha and Tom and her job and her memory and her body parts and her ability to bear children—even Emma would have been a more understandable choice. I could hear Ruth's incredulity like a loud laugh of surprise in that kitchen; I don't think I ever managed to satisfy the curiosity of my friends on the subject of Januscz and me.

I do remember that once when Ruth stopped over on a Friday morning in winter and Januscz was there with his coffee and his suit jacket and his tie and I was in my red sweater and tights, shoeless, sliding back and forth over the linoleum, I began to tell them both a story in an effort to break the silence. I have no idea why I picked the story I did, or what made me have that particular memory on that particular morning, but it was a story that I remember my great-great-grandmother telling herself in some aunt's kitchen in Virginia when I was little

yellow

enough to be sitting on someone's lap. It was a story about her great-great-grandmother's wedding and how orb-weaving spiders had been collected and placed around the gardens of the plantation house the night before the wedding to weave their webs and then in the early morning, when the dew was still on the webs and the air was still misty and foggy, the Negro houseservants had gone around and dusted them with gold pigment or powder so that when the sun shone at the party, the trees and the boxwood and the lilacs and shrubberies were all festooned with golden, shimmering webs. The bride herself had made this strange request.

When I finished telling the story, Ruth was laughing, but Januscz and I were both in tears and she soon left and I didn't see much of her after that until some time after Januscz had died, in fact. After that, we went back to being friends again in pretty much the old way we had of laughing a lot and talking about this and that, having coffee together. Whatever Ruth made of Januscz and me, she kept pretty much to herself.

Although Januscz and I never managed to get married or even to discuss marriage, he was the only man besides my father whom I managed to love until death. Physical death. Death of the body. I was experienced mainly in the death of love until Januscz came along. And that, I realize now, is such a controllable obsession. Love is. One, if one is like I used to be, enters into love with a death date already established, like the fifth act of a tragedy, so that in a curious way, the affair is conducted between two corpses, two already-dead people. But with Januscz, I forgot to set the date. And, when it came, as I must have known it would—Januscz was not a young man—it came in such a ridiculous way. We had been playing on a Sunday. He went away on business Monday morning. He died in his hotel room between Tuesday night and Wednesday morning and he never came back.

And so, what I remember is that we had been playing. We

had taken the boys for a picnic supper up north along the Delaware at Washington's Crossing. And Januscz played so hard with them, but not at football or soccer. He got the idea of raking all of the leaves into a huge pile. It was the last Sunday in October and most of the leaves were down. He instructed them in making rakes from branches, tying the larger, dead ones together with more flexible ones he cut with his pocket knife. And they all, all three of them, began raking and raking as if they would rake all the leaves in the forest into one mountain of leaves. And for the rest of the afternoon, they exhausted themselves with raking and flinging themselves onto the leaves.

When it was dark and there was only the light of our little fire and the play of moonlight on the river, Januscz sat next to me at the picnic table drinking a cup of boiled coffee from a tin camping mug and smoking a cigarette. The boys were still at the leaf pile, lying on their backs, counting stars, identifying the dipper, the hunter, and Cassiopeia, which I had taught them to see. They exclaimed at a shooting star. "Someone has died," Januscz called over to them and Jason, my little one, called back, "Where did they go?" "Down," answered Daniel, my eldest. "They fall down to earth." Januscz and I looked at each other and I began to clear the dishes away.

Yellow

WOMAN INSIDE THE WOMAN

■

Ivan Argüelles

there are others more like glass
who exist for the sake of frailty
there are some consumed with fire
who burn with pride and rage
and still others like painted fans
who turn casually in a tropic wind
for all of them desire is a moment
straddled to a plunging horse whose
exit is immediate through the golden noose
and nothing remains of that swift ride
but yearning and its thousand years
such women are pages in the Book
ciphers in the succession of thoughts
you live outside them all—the woman
inside the woman cathedral of salt
rebuilt daily upon the foaming wave
and around you the beasts fall hurtling
form the ark of incandescence and shame
lovers turn into photographs blazing
boats of dead husbands sink in flames—
this marvelous hell of smoke-stack lightning
which is your one and only presence!
you owe nothing and your debt is full!
a single cigarette and the sky ignites
into a paradise of blinded angels
among them you keep sweet favorites
of molten gold with crimson teeth
universes of dust precede you
through incarnations of lethal beauty
but you tower outside the world's
brief and trembling moment!

kingdom of the damned becomes bright
in recognition of your eyes
the infernal drum keeps pounding at the gate
and all those who mourned the lost
bring to their mouths the rose whose
black seed is heaven in you reborn

I know these things   I have been there

"All persuasions; no brutality."

NOTES ON THE CONTRIBUTORS

Sigmund Abeles received his MFA from Columbia University in 1957. After twenty-seven years of full-time teaching, he is buried in his studio working on new art, including many images of couples. He says, "Figures and faces alone motivate me to work . . . the coming together and separating of the flesh and the spirit seems to be the sub-theme of all my work." His work was featured in *Yellow Silk*, issue 26.

Ivan Argüelles works as a librarian at UC Berkeley, where he also coordinates the Morrison Room Poetry Series. His most recent poetry collections are *Baudelaire's Brain* and *Looking for Mary Lou: Illegal Syntax*, which received the Poetry Society of America's William Carlos Williams Award.

Ronald Baatz has published three books of poetry, including *All the Days Are* (Tideline Press) and *Strange Breakfast* (Permanent Press). He lives in upstate New York.

Jeffery Beam is a botanical librarian at UNC Chapel Hill and lives in rural North Carolina, where he and his lover "seek the reconciliation of opposites among their gardens and animals in an odd place named Golgonooza at Frog Level." His most recent books are *Midwinter Fires* (French Broad Press, 1989) and *The Fountain* (forthcoming).

Noelle Caskey recently completed her doctoral dissertation at UC Berkeley. Her poems have appeared in Italian and American journals and anthologies, and she has been in love with the same man for fifteen years.

Paul Castagna lives in northern Minnesota. When asked for biographical information, he said (in part), "Om Oasis Ashland Iron Wood Schools Prison Open Road . . . Hell Picasso Michelangelo Miles Beatles . . . New York Japan Paris Corsica . . . Glad To Have Been Born." His work was featured in *Yellow Silk*, issue 21.

Carole Chambers has lived on Hornby Island in British Columbia for the past fifteen years. Her first collection of poetry was *Still Life under the Occupation* (Quadrant Editions, Toronto, 1988).

Karen Chase has been poet-in-residence at the New York Hospital–Cornell Medical Center for the past ten years. Her work has appeared in numerous journals, including *Shenandoah*, *Caliban*, and *Exquisite Corpse*.

Sandra Russell Clark lives in New Orleans and began photographing in 1976. Since then, her work has appeared in such magazines as *Vogue* and *American Photographer*, and was featured in *Yellow Silk*, issue 28. Her photographs are shot with infrared film and hand-colored.

Wanda Coleman recently published a limited edition of love poems entitled *The Dicksboro Hotel and Other Travels* (Ambrosia Press, 1989). She lives in Los Angeles, where she is best known for her dramatic performances. Her other books include *Heavy Daughter Blues: Poems and Stories 1966–1986* (Black Sparrow Press).

Gina Covina's novel, *The City of Hermits* (Barn Owl Books), from which the story included here was excerpted, centers around a big San Francisco earthquake that hadn't yet happened when the book was published in 1983. Gina lives in Berkeley, California, where she writes about the natural world for the *East Bay Express*. Her watercolors of flowers appeared in *Yellow Silk*, issue 12.

Yellow

Elli Crocker, a native of Boston, received her MFA from Tufts in 1981 and is assistant professor of art at Clark University. Her work was featured in *Yellow Silk*, issue 29.

Steven DaGama lives in Cuyahoga Falls, Ohio, where he is currently completing his childhood memoir and a collection of new and selected poems. He has published four previous collections of poetry, and his work has been translated into five languages. He is also an artist, with paintings and drawings in public and private collections in the United States and Canada.

Judy Dater received her MFA from San Francisco State University and has been guest instructor at numerous universities in the United States, France, and Japan. She has published four books, including *Imogen Cunningham: A Portrait* and, most recently, *Body and Soul: Ten American Women* (with Carolyn Coman). Her work was featured in *Yellow Silk*, issue 7.

C. M. Decarnin is a radical feminist who believes that "the freedom to say Yes is as vital to growth as the freedom to say No, and that sexual repression must be recognized as a form of sexual abuse." Her work has appeared in many journals, including the original *Coming to Power*, *The Little Magazine*, and *Outrageous Women*. She is co-editor of the lesbian and gay science fiction anthology, *Worlds Apart* (Alyson Publications).

Ray Clark Dickson lives with his wife on a boat in the northern California delta. His poems have appeared in such journals as *Beloit Poetry Journal*, *The Smith*, and *River Rat Review*, and he has published one novel, *The Sound of Flowers*.

Miriam Dyak, in addition to writing poetry, teaches herbal healing, yoga, and womancraft in Seattle, Washington.

Anita Endrezze is half Yaqui Indian and half Rumanian, Italian, and Yugoslavian. Her work has appeared in many books and journals, including the *Anthology of 20th-Century NativeAmerican Poets*, and been translated into five languages. She is also a painter and storyteller.

Gary Epting is a painter and sculptor living in California. His erotica is in collections and has been published in Japan, Europe, and the United States. His drawings have appeared in *Yellow Silk*, issues 11, 14, and 19.

W. A. Fahey lives on Long Island Sound. His poems and stories have appeared in such journals as *Blue Unicorn* and *The Wormwood Review*. He is the author of *F. Scott Fitzgerald and the American Dream* and a forthcoming collection of poems, *Body Parts*.

Cerridwen Fallingstar has been a Wiccan priestess for fourteen years, and has published numerous articles, poems, and stories. Since its appearance in *Yellow Silk*, "Fiona McNair" has been revised and is part of her first novel, *The Heart of the Fire* (Cauldron Publications, 1990), which features Fiona as its main character, chronicling her growth and training as a young witch in sixteenth-century Scotland during the Burning Times.

David Fisher lives in Santa Rosa, California, and has ten children. His work has appeared in journals ranging from *Harper's* to *The Communist Daily Worker*. His book, *Teachings*, won the Poetry Society of America's William Carlos Williams Award in 1978, and *The Book of Madness* was nominated for a Pulitzer Prize in 1980.

Geoffrey Fox has written extensively on Latin American culture, including a collection of stories, *Welcome to My Contri* (Hudson View Press, 1988). "Dancing with Lucha" is part of an unpublished novel, *The Liberators*.

Marilyn Hacker is the author of six books of poetry, including *Going Back to the River* (Random House, 1990) and *Love, Death and the Changing of the Seasons* (Arbor House, 1986), a novel in sonnets about a passionate relationship between two women. She received the National Book Award in 1975 for *Presentation Piece*, and was, from 1982 through 1986, editor of the feminist literary magazine *13th Moon*.

Jane Hirshfield has received a Guggenheim Fellowship, the Commonwealth Club of California's 1988 Poetry Prize, and numerous other honors. Her work has appeared in *The New Yorker, Atlantic, American Poetry Review*, and the *Pushcart Prize Anthology*, among others, and her most recent books are *Of Gravity & Angels* (Wesleyan University Press, 1988) and *The Ink Dark Moon* (Scribners, 1988), a co-translation of ancient Japanese poetry.

Mikhail Horowitz is a performance poet of the neo-Beat/abstract depressionist persuasion, whose work has been seen in New York City, the Taos Poetry Festival, and luminous and sundry venues in the Hudson Valley, where he lives with a Pre-Raphaelite rock star, her dog, and nine cats. His book of collages and captions, *Big League Poets* (City Lights, 1978), is out of print in all the finest bookstores.

Jeannie Kamins lives in Montreal and has been an artist since 1974, when she "left her husband and got serious about ART." Originally a painter, she later worked with fabrics, then combined the two in a series of portraits done in fabric with faces and hands painted in oils. Her recent work has been more political, including the 1986 performance piece, "Amazing Grace." She was featured in *Yellow Silk*, issue 17.

Serge Kantorowicz was born and lives in Paris, and studied at the Ecole des Beaux-Arts de Bruxelles. His work has been shown throughout Europe, as well as in Argentina and the United States, and was featured in *Yellow Silk*, issue 32.

Rick Kempa teaches at Western Wyoming College. His first book of poems, *Making Light*, was published in 1989 by Mesilla Press.

SILK

William Kotzwinkle is the author of many unusual works, including the World Fantasy Award–winning novel *Dr. Rat* (Knopf, 1976). His stories have been collected in *Elephant Bangs Train* (Pantheon, 1971) and *Jewel of the Moon* (Putnam, 1985); his most recent book is *The Hot Jazz Trio* (Houghton-Mifflin, 1989).

Steve Kowit lives, teaches, and does animal rights work in San Diego. His poems inspired by the erotic poetry of India (*Srngararasa*, the "erotic mood," is one of the major divisions of Sanskrit poetry) have appeared in two collections, *Heart in Utter Confusion* (Dog Ear Press) and *Passionate Journey* (City Miner).

Betty LaDuke has traveled extensively in Third World countries, and her numerous publications include *Campaneras: Women, Art & Social Change in Latin America* (City Lights) and *Africa Through the Eyes of Women Artists* (Africa World Press, forthcoming). Her work was featured in *Yellow Silk*, issue 25.

Dorianne Laux lives in Berkeley, California, with the poet Ron Salisbury and her daughter, Tristem. Her first book of poetry, *Awake* (1990), has been published by BOA Editions as part of the New Poets of America series.

Michael Leu was born in Taiwan and currently resides in California. His early training in Chinese brush painting is still evident amidst the bright colors of his recent mixed-media work, which has been exhibited widely and was featured in *Yellow Silk*, issue 22.

Lynn Luria-Sukenick is associate professor at San Diego State University, has taught in the Poets-in-the-Schools program, and has a private practice in writing and healing. Her work has appeared in many magazines, and she has published four collections of poetry, including *Houdini Houdini* (Cleveland State University Press). She is currently completing a book of short stories.

yellow

Mary Mackey lives and works in California, where she is chair of the West Coast branch of PEN. She has published five novels and four books of poetry. Her most recent poetry collection is *The Dear Dance of Eros* (Fjord Press, Seattle).

Carole Maso is the author of *Ghost Dance* (1986), which incorporates the story included here, and *The Art Lover* (1990), both from North Point Press. She has just completed her third novel, *The American Woman in the Chinese Hat*.

Dan May earns his living as a full-time artist in Oakland, California. Encouraged from an early age by his parents, he is largely self-taught, and works mainly in painting, silkscreen, and monoprint. His work was featured in *Yellow Silk*, issue 10.

Rebecca Meketa lives with her husband, Dennis, and her children, Jarek and Madison, in Tijaras, New Mexico. She works as a sales representative because it allows her to "make money communicating—but the written word holds a deeper love." Previous publications include *Conceptions Southwest*. A Pueblo Indian once told her that her hair "drips fire."

Carolyn Miller is a free-lance book editor in San Francisco. She is currently working on a second poetry manuscript, looking for a publisher for the first, and "sort of copublishing a literary magazine."

Leslie Adrienne Miller teaches at the University of Houston, where she is a Ph.D. candidate in literature and creative writing. Her book, *Staying Up for Love*, is forthcoming from Carnegie-Mellon University Press.

John Minczeski is the author of two poetry collections, *The Spiders* and *The Reconstruction of Light*, and has edited several anthologies, including *Concert at Chopin's House: A Collection of*

Polish-American Writing (New Rivers Press). He lives in St. Paul, Minnesota, where he has worked in the Writers-in-the-Schools program.

Peter E. Murphy was born in Newport, Wales, and grew up in New York City. He teaches English at Atlantic City High School and Stockton State College, and his poetry has appeared in such journals as *Beloit Poetry Journal*, *Commonweal*, and *New York Quarterly*.

D. Nurkse has published work in *American Poetry Review* and *The Quarterly*, among others. His most recent book is *Shadow Wars* (Hanging Loose Press).

Mayumi Oda was born in a suburb of Tokyo and now resides in California. Her work has been shown in the United States and Japan, and was featured in *Yellow Silk*, issues 1 and 31, and on the cover of issue 8. She is the author of *Goddesses* (Volcano Press) and a children's book, *Happy Veggies* (Parallax).

Lance Olsen is the author of "one damn strange erotic novel," *Live from Earth* (Available Press), and two books on post-modern fiction. He's currently at work on a collection of stories called *Addicted to Love*, and a critical study of cyber-punk William Gibson. He teaches at the University of Kentucky.

Regina O'Melveny is a writer, assemblage artist, and homemaker. Her work has appeared in *Electrum*, *Jacaranda Review*, *Dreamworks*, *Iris*, and numerous other journals.

Phoebe Palmer lives in Cambria, California. Her main medium is oil painting, though she works with facility in steel and ferro-cement. Her formal education includes the University of Chicago and the Rhode Island School of Design; her informal education, working as a Pullman porter, a psychiatric aide, and a waitress. Her work was featured in *Yellow Silk*, issue 30.

Yellow

Noel Peattie is humanities librarian at UC Davis, and editor and publisher of *Sipapu*, a newsletter concerning the alternative press. The *Sipapu* anthology entitled *A Passage for Dissent* (McFarland, 1989) includes an interview with *Yellow Silk* editor/publisher Lily Pond.

Elaine Perry was born in Lima, Ohio, and now lives in New York City. Her first novel is *Another Present Era* (Farrar, Straus & Giroux, 1990).

Stephen John Phillips teaches photography at the Maryland Institute College of Art. His work has been published in *Zoom, American Photographer*, and *High Fashion Tokyo*, among others, and is in the collections of the National Museum of American Art, the Corcoran Gallery, and the Baltimore Museum. His photographs were featured in *Yellow Silk*, issue 27.

Marge Piercy is the author of eleven volumes of poetry, including *Available Light* (Knopf), and ten novels, the most recent being *Summer People* (Summit). She has also edited an anthology of contemporary American women's poetry, *Early Ripening*, published by Unwin Hyman.

Lily Pond has been editor, publisher, designer, production department, bookkeeper, and maid for *Yellow Silk* since February 29, 1981. She says, "Love is the only appropriate fetish."

Sarah Randolph earns her living as a papermaker in Provincetown, Massachusetts. Her work has appeared in many journals, including *The Quarterly, American Poetry Review*, and *Common Lives/Lesbian Lives*.

Donald Rawley is a poet, screenwriter, and journalist living in Los Angeles, where he is a private pupil of Kate Braverman. His poems are included in the anthology *American Poetry Confronts the 90s* (Black Tie Press). He has been in love with the same person for many years and hopes it will continue that way.

Bonnie Roberts is a poet-in-residence in the schools of Huntsville, Alabama. Her poems have appeared in such journals as *Croton Review*, *Kentucky Poetry Review*, and *Amelia*. She says, "For better or for worse, I have planted my feet in Southern soil and grow my poems here."

Peggy Roggenbuck (Gillespie) is a former actress who has worked as a psychotherapist with the terminally ill. In addition to her stories and poems, she has written numerous articles for such journals as *New Age* and *Yoga Journal*.

Michael Rosen lives in San Francisco, and has published two books of his own work, *Sexual Magic* (1986) and *Sexual Portraits: Photographs of Radical Sexuality* (1990). His work was featured in *Yellow Silk*, issue 5.

Richard A. Russo is a reference librarian for the Alameda (California) County Library System. He was guest editor for issue 24 of *Yellow Silk*, and has also edited an anthology of writings about dreams, entitled *Dreams Are Wiser Than Men* (North Atlantic, 1987). He writes science fiction under the name Richard Cornell.

Susan St. Aubin has published stories in such journals as *Short Story Review* and *Xanthippe*. Her erotic fiction has been included in the anthologies *Herotica* (Down There Press) and *Erotic by Nature* (Red Alder).

Charles Semones lives in a century-old farmhouse in the community where he was born, Harrodsburg, Kentucky. He is a former teacher who retired early to devote himself full-time to writing, and has published a collection of poetry, *Witch Cry* (Kentucky Poetry Press).

Ntozake Shange is a writer and performance artist whose most recent novel is *Betsy Brown* (St. Martin's, 1985). Her poetry is collected in *Nappy Edges* (St. Martin's, 1978) and she is the author of the "choreopoem," *for colored girls who have considered suicide/when the rainbow is enuf* (1975).

Marilyn Sides teaches at Wellesley College. "The Island of the Mapmaker's Wife" was her first published story and was selected for inclusion in the *1990 O. Henry Prize Collection*.

Robert Silverberg has written or edited over a hundred books of fiction and non-fiction, including the Nebula Award–winning science fiction novel *A Time of Changes* (1975). "Thesme and the Ghayrog" is taken from the middle volume of the trilogy that consists of *Lord Valentine's Castle* (1980), *Majipoor Chronicles* (1982), and *Valentine Pontifex* (1983).

Gary Soto is associate professor of Chicano Studies and English at UC Berkeley, and the author of six volumes of poetry, the most recent being *Who Will Know Us?* (Chronicle Books, 1990). He has also published several volumes of occasional essays and prose recollections, including *Living Up the Street* (1985), *Small Faces* (1986), and *Lesser Evils* (1988).

Arlene Stone has published six books, and two plays, *A Ladies' Room* and *Hag*, in addition to numerous poems, essays, and stories. She lives in San Francisco.

Roberta Swann is co-founder of the American Jazz Orchestra and program director of The Great Hall at The Cooper Union in New York City. Her poetry and fiction have appeared in such journals as *Ploughshares* and *North American Review*.

Joy Tremewan produces and hosts a radio book-review program in Memphis, Tennessee. Her work has appeared in *Asylum*, *Radiance*, and *Memphis Magazine*.

Jane Underwood lives with her seven-year-old son, two cats, and two goldfish in California, and earns her living as a free-lance writer. Her most recent work has appeared in *Five Fingers Review*, *Mirage*, and *HOW(ever)*.

SILK

Harry Weisburd received his MFA from the California College of Arts and Crafts and resides in Oakland. He has worked in a variety of media, including painting, drawing, and film. His work was featured in *Yellow Silk*, issue 20. He also did a collaborative piece with Arlene Stone in issue 15.

Sarah Brown Weitzman won an NEA Fellowship in 1984 and has published poetry in such journals as *Croton Review*, *Poet & Critic*, and *Kansas Quarterly*.

Roberta Werdinger is currently completing her masters in creative writing at San Francisco State University, where she received the Academy of American Poets award in 1989.

Jeffrey Wilson was born in Oakland, has an MFA in writing from the California College of Arts and Crafts, and is a park ranger in northern California.

Ira Wood teaches screenwriting at writers' conferences throughout the country, and is the author of a play, *The Last White Class* (with Marge Piercy), and a novel, *The Kitchen Man* (1987). His new novel will appear in spring 1991.

Elaine Perez Zickler teaches part-time and is finishing her Ph.D. at Bryn Mawr College. Her poetry has appeared in such journals as *Aileron Press* and *South Coast Poetry Review*, and she has completed her first novel.